Handling Business

DeVonshae Ali

Copyright © 2017 DeVonshae Ali: Authentic Life Instructions

All rights reserved.

ISBN: 13: 978-1546649519
ISBN-10: 1546649514

DEDICATION

This book is dedicated to single mothers who sacrifice daily to provide for their children. I know it's hard to be the head of a household while working, going to school and trying to find a few minutes for your own sanity. God is with you through the struggle. Don't lose faith because little eyes are watching you. Psalm 27: 13-14, "I would have lost heart, unless I had believed that I would see the goodness of the Lord in the land of the living. Wait on the Lord, be of good courage, and HE shall strengthen your heart. Wait, I say on the Lord!"

CONTENTS

1. FAITH UNDER FIRE
2. CATCHING HELL
3. MIRROR, MIRROR
4. WALK ON WATER
5. HOPE WILL HEAL
6. VISION IS CLEAR
7. NO MORE TEARS
8. LOVE ME NOW
9. SUNSHINE

Handling Business

Handling Business

ACKNOWLEDGMENTS

God is my source. He has given me victory in every area of my life. My strength comes from daily conversations with my Creator. I am thankful for Elijah, Isaiah and Joshua. Thank you to everyone who loves and prays for me. I appreciate you for supporting my dreams.

I want to acknowledge the Jennings Warriors c/o 87 & 88. Our alumni have become closer over the years. I appreciate the cheers, encouragement and support that you give to me and my sons. Power of Unity International, I am grateful for our Morning Prayer sessions and times of fasting. I have been strengthened in my Christian walk. Many of you pour into my life regularly. To Tiffany Rodney, you are a true example of a faithful friend. No matter what is going on in your own life you make sure to inquire about my health and wellbeing. You just don't know what that means to me. Grandpa Eddie Rider, may you rest in peace. I have never met a man of your caliber! I pray that my sons grow up to be just as accepting, loving and godly. To my parents, George & Jeanne Dyson, I hope that you are proud of all my accomplishments. To my grandmother, Annie Mae, I cling to your wisdom taught to me through song… "You can't hurry God O' know, you just have to wait. You have to trust Him and give Him time, no matter how long it takes. He's a God you can't hurry. He will be there, you don't have to worry. He may not come when you want Him, but He's right on time."

All praises to the on time God!

Handling Business

1 FAITH UNDER FIRE

Three years is a long time to love someone, even if it's not a perfect love. Then again, can love ever be perfect when it is attempted by two imperfect people?

It was the first Friday night that Ty'nae would spend without Ryan. She longed for a Mojito to calm her nerves. The Cuban rum would be sure to relax her and at least for a while drive the melancholy blues away. Even during their relationship ups and downs, movie night had been a special time that they both looked forward to and Ty'nae wouldn't soon let go of the memories. Movie night alone was tormenting to say the least. She recalled the big, green quilt with a yellow Packers' football helmet that Ryan's mom made him when he was away at college. It would keep their bodies warm as they ate buttered popcorn and red Kool-Aid with lots of sugar. Ty'nae was a mobster movie buff and Ryan loved old, western, cowboy movies. Each of them would grin and bear the other's choices. Without Ryan's presence on this Friday night, the house they'd been living in for only a short while was quiet. His absence was an open wound that only the Balm of Gilead could heal. Ty'nae was depressed. Every now and then you could hear an occasional coo from their baby girl, Stormy. That wasn't enough to replace the void of Ryan's presence. It was only adding insult to injury. The place felt empty and Ty'nae's heart was in mourning over the unexpected death of her relationship with Ryan. She was devastated and felt a void that just wouldn't fade away.

Ty'nae paced the hardwood floors of her home back and forth for hours in disbelief as she held her baby close. Once Stormy fell asleep, Ty'nae laid her gently in a cozy cherry wood crib on her side and stood over her taking in her every physical feature. At three months old, Stormy had more hair than Ty'nae who wore hers in a short, sassy, blond afro. Stormy's soft, sandy brown ringlets overpowered her infant sized face. Ty'nae rubbed the back of her hand across her daughter's cheek and allowed a tear she was holding hostage to finally go free. One tear was followed by many more that had been awaiting their turn to run down the smooth, mocha colored, face of a woman scorned. Ty'nae repented silently for feelings of resentfulness; Stormy looked more like Ryan. Looking at his spitting image only made the pain in Ty'nae's heart hurt worse. It was a sharp stabbing pain that made it hard to take each breath. Ryan's Irish side gave Stormy a tinge of redness to her complexion and a few faint freckles. His Italian blood contributed to the bone structure of her nose. His Native American ethnicity had contributed to the big heap of shiny hair on Stormy's head.

Although Ryan's father was African American, nothing but Stormy's grandmother's DNA was obvious to the eye. Ty'nae had simply birthed her, but none of her or her family could be seen in the child's physical features. Ty'nae had hoped to pass on her own full lips, big brown eyes and thick eyebrows but God had other plans.

Thoughts of a make-over ran across Ty'nae's mind as she caught a slight glimpse of herself in a nearby wall mirror. A new sew-in with blonde highlights and freshly arched eyebrows is what she longed to have for her beautification. She knew it was only a thought because the lack of time and money was her new normalcy as a single mom.

Ty'nae rolled a pink, fluffy blanket and used it to prompt Stormy comfortably in the middle of the crib before walking out of the room and heading to the kitchen. She ignored the dishes piled in the sink and the stench of dirty pampers in the trash can. She double checked the back door to ensure it was locked, lowered the blinds to the window that overlooked the backyard and reached into the cabinet for a wine glass. She opened the stainless steel refrigerator and for a moment forgot what she was looking for. She retrieved a bowl of cherries covered in plastic wrap and before placing it on the counter went back to get the bottle of Moscato wine she'd planned to finish off. It wouldn't do the same trick as a shot of whiskey but it was time for something more than the Mojito. She was glad to sip on anything that could drive her sorrow away. Ty'nae sat up to the marble counter with both of her bare feet dangling from a bar stool. The chipped, red polish on her toes were a tale tell sign that being a new mom left no time to pamper herself. Although she had given up smoking soon as she found out she was pregnant, she longed to have a Salem Lights cigarette between her full lips. She poured her drink in a fancy glass, took a sip and hung her head in her hand to sob once more. She couldn't believe Ryan had walked out on her and Stormy. Theirs was a tumultuous relationship, but she hadn't expected him to just up and disappear. At times, Ty'nae pondered upon how her child's name surely summed up the last three years of her love life. She had named her daughter after a childhood friend, but Ty'nae's life had been nothing short of stormy since Ryan had proved to be unstable.

Ty'nae knew God was never pleased with her shacking up with Ryan in the first place, but things had happened between them so fast and before she knew it she was all caught up. Three years prior, Ty'nae had been so bored with life she felt like dying. Moving to St. Louis had not been as promising as she'd thought. She didn't know anyone and other than work, Ty'nae had no social life. Although she left Memphis in order to start a new job, the moment reality set in she found herself all alone in a new city that wasn't friendly towards her. St. Louis was more racially divided than she had expected. She wanted to experience diversity. She wanted to have a melting pot of friends. She wanted to go to a multicultural church. Ty'nae decided to turn to the internet in order to meet people and possibly make a love connection. She placed a profile on an online dating site and met Ryan within a few weeks of searching through internet rubbish. She would never attempt online dating again. She was so fed up with names like Big Trigger, Suck Hard, Thrills 4 Bills, and Donkey Dick. It was disgusting. The men were overweight, missing teeth and many simply were trying to play women for fools. She heard the craziest stories, chatted with men who ended up being married and was tired of men asking if she'd perform phone sex. Many of the men had proved to be liars. Most men claiming to live in gated communities were prisoners. She tried to be smart about it, but still she would find the Freddy Krueger's of internet dating. She checked all the men's identities out using a website called Don't Date'em Girl. Soon, she learned how to dig deeper on the Missouri Case Net and sex offender websites. She also figured out other sites that found information on crimes committed, taxes paid on property and other important factors. She'd discovered child predators, men with fake careers and stolen identities that matched someone else's picture to their name. Some of the people had had sex changes and it was a cesspool of crazy guys with weird sexual preferences. Every now and then she would meet a real straight up man with no ill intentions, but the conversation would be so boring that Ty'nae could hear crickets in the background. Then, one day she got an inbox from a man that wanted to hold an intelligent conversation. He wasn't the best looking man in her opinion but his intelligence was a big turn on. Although he was of a mixed race, she didn't mind at all. They chatted on line for weeks before talking on the phone. Although she had not initially been attractive to him the conversations drew them closer and closer. They finally agreed to meet at a local Starbucks. She remembered the gray pants he wore with a starched white shirt covered by a blue polo vest. He looked like a school teacher with his glasses on, but once he started talking his personality came through.

Ryan was charismatic, smelled good and had a way with words. Ty'nae assessed him as an easily likable guy with dry humor and an extensive knowledge about politics. Ryan worked as a car dealer and had dreams of opening his own small lot. He'd already obtained a dealership license and used it to go to auctions were he could find reasonable deals to build his car inventory. Most of the cars he owned, he kept at his friends family's farm.

Both Ryan and his friend Sam loved cars more than anything. Ryan talked about his frequent trips to the farm. Ty'nae was happy to find someone she could talk to about trading her Mazda in for a Camry. Ryan's charm and knowledge of cars got to her in a way that she'd never imagined. She loved hearing him go on and on about politics. She grew to like him an awful lot. He was the reason that she had started listening to NPR for political updates. He was her reason to start changing her diet as he was a health nut. They started going to the movies weekly and attended a few car shows and auctions. She finally got the car she wanted and was glad Ryan had handled all the paperwork and landed her a great deal. Then, they soon began rotating between each other's homes for movie night every Friday. As things progressed they started going to church every Sunday at Ty'nae's suggestion, although Ryan didn't claim to be a Christian. He went along with it mostly out of curiosity since Ty'nae seemed so passionate about church attendance.

Ryan had always prided himself on his high sex drive and bedroom performance. He found Ty'nae extremely attractive and her body made it hard for him to not want to take things further. Ty'nae had full lips that made kissing extremely erotic. She could walk into a room with happy eyes, an alluring smile and fly blond afro and leave a memorable impression. Her strong presence and big booty made Ryan want to undress her anytime and anyplace. He longed to lick her flesh and hear her scream in ecstasy. He soon started making sexual advancements towards her and her once strong faith was compromised. Her talks of abstaining from sex until marriage started to be a big issue between them. Ryan also would say mean things about Ty'nae's smoking habit. He couldn't see why she had strong views on abstinence but not smoking. He absolutely detested smoking. Ty'nae tried to explain that she was praying for deliverance from smoking but words like, 'deliverance', 'repentance' and 'Christianity' aggravated Ryan who thought it was all crazy talk. He would say, "You sound like the church folks who think they can pray being gay away." Ty'nae hated when he said that because she truly believed that God could indeed help people battling with same sex addiction break free and she trusted that God would break the chain of nicotine addiction in her own life.

Ty'nae tried to resist sex with Ryan because of her strong religious views but even when they were arguing all she could think about was sexing him. She could only focus on being set free from one thing at a time. She was a piece of work that God would have to totally gut out like a house and rebuild from the bottom. During a movie night at Ryan's place things got heated and before long Ty'nae had come undone. Ryan's lips knew no limits and her entire body felt the softness of his warm tongue on her flesh. His scent was different from other men she'd known intimately in her past and it soon became an aphrodisiac. The passion between them was an inferno that took them both to the edge and it was only outside of the bed that they could not stand each other. Her mouth irked him and his mood swings angered her. It had only taken two months to realize that they didn't know each other well enough to be fornicating but, the sex was too good to let go. Ty'nae started spending more and more time at Ryan's and before long she was living there. A year into their relationship Ryan told Ty'nae that he wanted out of their live in arrangement and she was heartbroken. He was fed up with her nicotine addiction and all they did was argue. Ty'nae had grown to love Ryan in her own way in spite of their daily disagreements about money, chores, and irritating habits. Ty'nae knew a break up was probably best for both of them but, sex had a hold on them and the chemistry made it hard for them to part ways. Every day she tried to gain the will to leave and she tried to convince herself that she would but couldn't. Ryan would make declarations of being over her on a daily basis, but not once did he make good on his threats to leave.

There were times they both wanted the other gone and as more and more red lights started to show, Ty'nae wanted to pray but felt so far from God she couldn't bring herself to bow in His presence. She knew that prodigals could always come home with open arms; however, the guilt of her sin was overwhelming. Ryan started becoming demanding and when she would not comply with his wishes he'd become verbally abusive. Then out of the blue he quit his job in pursuit of starting an off the wall vitamin water business and Ty'nae was left to pay the bills alone. Ty'nae was noticing that Ryan had some deeply embedded anger issues. She wanted him to seek help, however, the thought of how he would react if asked to seek counseling made her shun away from the subject. His mood swings were irritating. It was such a struggle never knowing what bag he would come out of and it seemed as if Ryan was all about himself. His sporadic behaviors worked Ty'nae's nerves, but the selfishness is what turned her completely off. She tried to talk to him about selling some of his cars, since he seemed to no longer be interested in starting a car lot, but that would get Ryan so heated that Ty'nae stopped mentioning it. She walked around on egg shells, afraid to piss him off and not wanting any negative confrontation with him. Ryan would only do minimum and seemed to always find money for the things that mattered to him. Ty'nae feared they would lose everything. As time went on, Ty'nae felt used. Ryan would stay gone for long hours and when he would get home he would be cold towards her and his eyes would be red. Yet, he always came to bed greedy. He'd devour her body, ravish her heart and with his meaty throbbing manhood he would stroke her right until she forgot about all of his wrongs. It really surprised her that when she got pregnant, Ryan actually seemed so happy. Ryan's entire attitude changed towards her and for once he started acting like he genuinely cared for her. Ty'nae had fantasies of them being a real family and forming a partnership to raise their child. She longed to do anything to make their relationship work. She wanted to believe it would all eventually work out with them. After all, she didn't want a child by a man that didn't care for her. Ryan started acting like a family man. He would go to doctor appointments with Ty'nae. He stopped staying out as late and coming home with bloodshot red eyes. Then, he found a new job at another car dealership, moved them into a bigger house and soon started talking about committing his life to God and doing things God's way. Ty'nae was glad he was back in the car business and really hoped he would go back to his dream of starting his own dealership. She was waving good bye to all the vitamin water ideas Ryan had been stuck on for way too long.

A few months into the pregnancy Ryan asked Ty'nae to marry him. She wore the dainty engagement ring with its gold band and emerald gemstone with pride. She wanted her family back in Memphis to see that she was doing well with a good job and engaged to be married. She felt they would be more accepting of her pregnancy since she was planning to officially wed her baby daddy. Things seemed to be finally perfect. She was happy and looked forward to having a small, intimate wedding with only their families shortly after Stormy was born. However, no sooner than the baby came home from the hospital did Ryan revert back to his cold hearted ways.

Ty'nae spent so much time crying over their relationship that she hadn't had a chance to fully enjoy becoming a mother. The last three months had been stressful as Ty'nae was adjusting to having a new baby. Ryan was moody, the house was unorganized and Ty'nae longed for a full night of sleep. Ty'nae was feeling blue. Down in the dumps wasn't far enough to explain all the emotions gripping at her heart and Ryan showed no compassion. Ryan acted unaffected by his baby girl. He barely held her, changed her or tried to bond with her. Ty'nae was overwhelmed and all her faith in Ryan and God were gone. Yet, she tried to tell herself that things would get better.

Ryan's behavior made Ty'nae feel insecure. Then, she arrived home one Wednesday from taking Stormy to the pediatrician for a check up to see that Ryan had taken most of his clothes and a few of his personal belongings and was gone. No note, no explanation or nothing. He was gone…vanished. Ty'nae was left in a house she couldn't afford and the place looked like a pigsty. There she was alone with a baby she hadn't planned to raise alone. She took off her ring which no longer seemed to promise commitment and wished she'd never met Ryan. Life seemed to be on a constant downward spiral. Ty'nae had missed work since she had no babysitter and was so worried about childcare for Stormy that she kept feeling on the verge of an anxiety attack.

So on the first Friday without Ryan she was drinking her sorrows away. The tears would fall into her wine glass as she put it to her lips to sip, but it didn't matter to her. Tears were at least a temporary relief from the pain that stabbed deep into her heart and the uncertainties that were tormenting her mind. A baby sitter for Stormy would at least calm her worries about her job. Her six weeks maternity leave had been over and Ryan's flexible work schedule had at least made it possible for her to return to work. Ty'nae would be on edge all day from worrying about her daughter in Ryan's care. However, he was Stormy's father, and her only option. Without him, what would she do for a babysitter. Ty'nae was willing to use the little sick and personal time she had left available in order to stay home and pick up the pieces of her broken life, but with a newborn she needed those days for doctors' visits and other unexpected emergencies. Going back to Memphis wasn't an option she wanted to consider. After all, she didn't want to go back home with a baby and no husband. Her family and their moral opinions would soon drive her to cussing.

Ty'nae nursed her drink mingled with the salt of her tears as she took notice of the signs that Ryan once lived in the house too. His bottle of wheat grass sat on the counter by his Nutribullet Pro 900 and Ty'nae noticed the spilled flaxseed around the base of it. She still hadn't gotten around to cleaning up the place the way it needed to be done. Ryan was ever the health food enthusiast but he wouldn't clean up behind himself. She looked up at the shiny handles he had recently put on all the cabinets to give them a more contemporary look. She could at least be grateful that he'd done that finally after months of her nagging. She stared at the burnt orange accent wall they had argued about when they first decorated the kitchen together. The paint color reminded her that Ryan always got his way. He'd even insisted on adding orange to the living room by putting orange and brown polka dot pillows on the couch. She hated the color orange but, she gave in to his demands to keep the peace.

Ty'nae sat on the bar stool for nearly an hour before she heard the sound of cooing coming from Stormy's room. She wanted to ignore it at first. She wanted to not be the one responsible for all of Stormy's needs. However, this new normalcy was hers alone to embrace. Ty'nae made her way to Stormy's room and looking into her daughter's bright eyes she knew that she had to be strong and find courage from deep within. She couldn't just assume Ryan would come back so she had to prepare to move forward without him. She took her baby girl and held her close to her chest. She inhaled the infant's scent, took notice of her milky breath and soft skin then, rubbed her curly hair. Ty'nae walked to the rocking chair in the corner of the room and sat down comfortably. As she rocked her baby she prayed, "God, it's been a long time but I really need you. Please help me. Please, please, please help me. I repent Lord. I am so sorry for my sins. I am far from the peaceful shore. I need you God." In all sincerity she cried out for God. Her faith was under fire and she needed God to restore her soul.

2 CATCHING HELL

Days had passed by without any sign of Ryan's return. Ty'nae didn't know what to do. She called her co-worker, Susan, for help. Susan was a mother of three adorable girls and Ty'nae admired how organized she was. She was also grateful for all the hand-me-down clothes Susan gave her for Stormy, as well as a car seat. Ty'nae held Stormy in one hand and tried to keep her calm while dialing Susan's number with her black, Nexus 2 cellphone. Susan answered in her always chipper voice.

"Hello", she said so happily that Ty'nae could see her smiling through the phone.

"Hello Susan. It's Ty'nae. Hate to disturb you on a Sunday."

"O' it's just fine. How's the baby?" Susan asked

"She's fine. Actually, that's why I'm calling. I want to know if you can recommend anyone who could babysit Stormy. Ryan left on an emergency business trip and it has been one complication after the other. I am not sure when he will get back. I'm in a real bind for Monday. I actually should consider a full time sitter because I can't chance more business trips like this coming up, you know." Ty'nae hated to lie but she didn't want anyone at work to know that Ryan had walked off and left her with a three month old baby. With all that was within her she tried to sound convincing.

"Sure, I understand. My husband and I had to get childcare pretty early on ourselves. I couldn't juggle the girls and a career without my sitter." Susan said.

"I have a regular sitter and a backup person. Currently my back up is seeking new clients. Only problem is that she's out of town until Thursday, and I'm sure you would love her."

Ty'nae took the sitter's name and phone number. She felt sad because she needed someone to watch Stormy ASAP. Ty'nae had already promised her boss she'd facilitate a meeting on Monday. She couldn't miss any more work. She wanted to see Ryan, to talk to him, to curse at him. How could he just walk away leaving her to fend for herself with his baby to care for alone? Ty'nae grabbed a bottle she had warmed earlier and sat on the tan couch in her living room. She used the orange and brown polka dot pillows to support her back and held the bottle to Stormy's mouth. She watched as Stormy put her hand to the bottle and kicked her little feet with joy. She was a happy little baby. Ty'nae smiled and for a moment lost herself in Stormy's eyes. In Stormy's eyes, Ty'nae saw love and for that moment Ryan became irrelevant. She was thankful for her child. The only thing that mattered was finding a way to make life work for her and her baby. However, the thought of single motherhood terrified her. She hadn't planned to do parenting a baby solo.

It was Sunday, so Ty'nae made a spare of the moment decision to go to church. She figured she needed to be in God's house because sitting in her own house was only making her more and more sad. She multitasked to get Stormy and herself presentable enough to walk into eleven o'clock service at North County Christian Church. She always felt welcome amongst the diversity of people and admired the churches acceptance of the many interracial couples who attended their services. She was even more appreciative that the church had a beautiful nursery.

When she arrived at the church, she was greeted by volunteers on the parking lot that helped her and baby Stormy get safely into the building. A church usher handed her a program and inquired if she knew where the nursery was located. Ty'nae thanked the usher, assured her that she knew her way around the building fairly well and made her way down to the corridor that led to the nursery. The walls were bright and filled with art work from the preschool department. Flyers where everywhere announcing a school supply drive for the churches back to school celebration. It seemed like the children in her community had just got out for summer break and it was already time to start thinking about school starting back up in August. She made a mental note to mark August 9th on her calendar so that she could attend the back to school program. Before she reached the nursery she saw Renee, one of the women she had met at bible study. Renee wore long, black Malaysian weave down her back and a gold, thin braided rope around her forehead that tied in the back and made her look like a black version of Pocahontas. Renee was 6 feet tall and had a body like a Victoria Secretes model. She had milk chocolate complexion, almond shaped eyes and perfectly straight white teeth. It was obvious to see that Renee loved her hips. She was always putting her hands on them. Ty'nae and Renee had quickly hit it off as they were both girly girls ever complimenting one another on their fashion sense. Sometimes, they would sit next to each other in bible class when Ty'nae went without Ryan. Ty'nae felt a little uncomfortable in Renee's presence on this particular Sunday as she had thrown on anything in order to get out of the house to church. Dark denims cuffed at the bottom with a pair of black pumps, a white t-shirt with the word, 'Flawless' across the front and black sweater she'd tied around her waist to hide her big booty and for later to help handle the coldness of the sanctuary. Ty'nae had a large diaper bag instead of a purse. She didn't have on her normal make up and earrings, but she was there to worship. Renee hugged her and stepped back to get a better look. She had a look on her face as if she was trying to figure something out, but she just smiled. She studied Ty'nae's face and knew that something wasn't right. Ty'nae could tell she was trying to figure out why she looked so half-done which was out of the norm.

"Hey Hun! Love ya, love ya, love ya! How are you babe?" Renee said smiling as she hugged Ty'nae once again and kissed the baby in her arms on the forehead.

"A little tired but all is well." Ty'nae didn't want to disclose the hell she was really going through.

"This child needs to let me get some rest." She laughed as she bounced Stormy a little as she talked.

"Girl, I know what you mean. I have been watching my niece for the last month and that child never sleeps!" Renee shook her head and put her right hand on her right hip dramatically.

"Your niece? You don't work during the day?" Ty'nae asked.

"Well, that's a long story, girlfriend." Renee said and this time she put her other hand on her other hip as well.

"All I can say is be careful what you pray for girl! I told God I wanted to be free to do what I always dreamt about and the next thing I knew my job downsized and I was unemployed. So, I decided to start Praise Kids Daycare. I only have my two year old niece and one other kid that comes only on Tuesday and Thursday, but God will send me more children I'm sure!"

Ty'nae stood there looking at Renee in shock. She started to tear up and Renee was confused.

"Wait love…what's wrong? Are you okay babe? Talk to me." Renee took Stormy out of Ty'nae's arms and she rubbed Ty'nae's back to comfort her.

"Let's get the baby into the nursery love and then we can talk." Renee motioned for Ty'nae to start walking towards the nursery. She was confused as to why Ty'nae had started to cry. After all, they hadn't known each other real long and only on a church basis, but she thought Ty'nae would be happy to hear that she had started her dream business. Renee handled signing Stormy into the nursery, got a name tag with child identification number on it and helped to put it on Ty'nae. She took her sister in Christ hand and led her to the area where coffee and light refreshments were sold before service.

"Would you like hot chocolate or coffee?" Renee asked Ty'nae as she also reached on the counter for tissue so that Ty'nae could wipe the tears still flowing down her face.

Through sniffles, Ty'nae managed to request hot chocolate and Renee put in an order for two cups. Renee reached into a small, tan, Coach cross bag and pulled out two wrinkled dollar bills to pay for the hot chocolate. She carried both cups to the nearest empty seats she could find and placed both cups on the table. They sat down and Renee pulled her long Malaysian weave behind her ears, crossed both hands in prayer position and began to pray softly.

"Dear God, I thank you for allowing me and Ty'nae to cross paths this morning. I trust that you ordained this for both of us. 'My sister's tears matter to you and I pray that during our time of fellowship you will dry those tears and replace them with your joy in Jesus name. Amen."

"Amen." Ty'nae said softly as she wiped yet another tear and blew into her cup before taking a sip of hot chocolate. The sweet, warm liquid felt good on her tongue and she let out a sigh.

Renee didn't say a word. She just sat there allowing the Holy Spirit to be the guide. Neither one of them seemed to know where to begin the conversation. Each looked around the room at others coming in and out to make purchases and a few rushing to get to the main sanctuary.

Finally, Renee reached for Ty'nae's hand and said, "What's going on sis? These tears can't be about my new daycare. Talk to me." She searched Ty'nae's face for clues. She didn't want to force it but, she was genuinely concerned about her sister in Christ.

"I feel like God is punishing me…" Ty'nae sobbed.

"I know I disobeyed him by moving in with Ryan, fornicating and getting pregnant out of wedlock." She took the crumbled up tissue and patting her eyes and cheeks. I have told God that I am sorry, but I don't feel forgiven. I feel lost. I am scared.

"Go on sis…" Renee encouraged her to keep talking.

"He left me! He left me and my baby! We are all alone. I have no family here. I don't know how I'm going to be able to work when I don't even have a babysitter. The one my co-worker recommended is out of town and I need to go to work tomorrow." Ty'nae head dropped. She felt so ashamed for bearing her soul. She worried that Renee would judge her. In her eyes, Renee had it all together; beauty, brains and a body to get any man she wanted.

Renee smiled. She sensed the Lord's presence at work. She felt Him at the table with them.

Renee was slow and careful with her words making sure to follow the Lord's leading. "Ty'nae, when I first came here to First Christian, I was out of touch with God. I was lost. I was hurting. I didn't have anyone to talk to about the mess my life was in at the time. See, my mom was never there for me. My sister and I lived a hard life. I was rapped at age 11 by my uncle. For as long as I could remember, life was the color black for me until I met my ex-husband. He is the only person who ever really loved me, but my pain wouldn't let me love him back the way that he deserved. I started coming here to church regularly, attended bible class and then one day I just surrendered. I got baptized. I stopped fighting and just let God take all of my problems. I was fornicating. To be blunt, I was whoring around big time."

Renee's mind went back to a time she only talked about when the spirit of God prompted her. Her testimony wasn't one that could be easily swallowed by others. She hesitated before speaking again, and then she took a deep breath, and proceeded telling her truth. She knew that God had his reasons for putting her in Ty'nae's presence.

"I left my husband for a man I met at work. I destroyed my family while I was out living like a wild child. I was hanging out in clubs, going to swinger's coffee shops like Shameless Grounds, dabbling in all sorts of perverseness. I was sleeping with married men for money. During the Mardi Gras weekend, I'd participate in the Naughti Gras event at Koken Art factory allowing myself to be inebriated in sexual sin. The devil had me so turned out Ty'nae, I couldn't function without sex. The woman you see today is not the woman I use to be. I was on my way to hell! I ended up losing my only son to suicide at the age of 14 because he was so hurt about my shameful lifestyle. He had no clue of all the other ungodly things I was doing. His dad tried to shield him from it all, but what he did know was eating him up inside while I was out in the streets acting like an idiot! I started snorting cocaine and just living a life with no respect for God. I lost my son and a man that loved me with every fabric of his being. I took his heart and stomped on it! He had never done wrong by me and yet in my sinfulness I broke his heart."

Renee shook her head in disbelief of how messed up her life once had been. She didn't care if Ty'nae thought less of her because she knew God had been faithful, kind and merciful to her and she owed it to Him to testify.

Ty'nae sat listening and felt bad that she had assumed life was so perfect for Renee when actually she had lived through so much darkness.

"Jesus loves us. It doesn't matter what we find ourselves in. When we are ready to come out he will deliver us." Renee assured.

"Deliverance." Ty'nae spoke the word as if her very life depended on it.

"Deliverance is what I need right now. I've been craving a cigarette so bad and all this stress is making it hard for me not to go buy a pack of Salem Lights even though I haven't had one since I got pregnant with Stormy. My heart is so broken. How could Ryan just leave without any explanation? How can I raise Stormy alone? How can I be delivered from all of this pain? I feel like I'm catching hell Renee. Pure hell!"

Renee smiled and her pretty white teeth shined as she spoke. "Girl, if God can deliver me from a sex addiction that had me out here living like a whore…excuse my French…he can deliver you from smoking and he sure can help you handle your business raising Stormy all by yourself!" She laughed. Renee just kept it 100% with Ty'nae. She wasn't the type to put on airs and act holier than thou.

"As far as Ryan is concerned, looks like God has already delivered you by letting him leave you. God obviously did you a favor! Just accept it.

Don't go looking for him. You have to let God deal with him. When someone walks out of your life, trust me, they are only making room for your blessings! Just work on you!"

Ty'nae smiled. She felt at ease with Renee. She kept looking at how beautiful Renee was and wondering what had drove her into the arms of so many different men and made her leave her husband. She could understand the disconnect Renee felt from her mom. Honestly, Ty'nae felt similar towards her dad who was never in her life. Ty'nae also wondered if Renee's transparency was God's way of showing her that all really do sin and fall short of God's glory. Ty'nae had so many questions, but she wouldn't violate her friend by prying further than she had already revealed. With all the media attention geared toward sex, it was hard to abstain. She knew that personally. Ty'nae had made it a practice to love everyone even if she didn't like the decisions they made for their own lives. She was in no place to judge. Her life was shipwrecked. It wasn't any of her business how Renee had lived in the past for real and she was happy Renee had survived her storm. To look at her you'd never guess that she'd endured so much pain and loss. Ty'nae prayed that God would have mercy and get her through the storm of life she was currently facing. After hearing Renee's testimony, Ty'nae knew that God was able.

"I'm sorry about your son and all…" Ty'nae said sincerely. "I'm sure you're still healing from that."

"Actually, I'm good now. At first, I was in a bad head space, but look what the Lord has done, honey child!" She smiled brightly and struck a pose in her chair with hands on hips.

"Looks like service is about to start, let's get in there." Renee said.

"O' by the way, you can drop Stormy off to me in the morning. Don't worry about paying. I will keep her until you can figure things out." Renee stood to hug Ty'nae and gathered their paper cups and napkins for the trash.

"Are you sure?" Ty'nae asked. "I don't want to be a burden, but Lord knows I came here today heavy in my spirit not knowing what I would do about childcare. I really do need to go to work tomorrow."

"Looks to me that why you were trying to figure it out, the Lord had already worked it out! It's no problem. I would love to care for Stormy." Renee said.

They embraced one last time and both of them begin to praise and worship God as they drew strength from one another. They walked into the sanctuary ready to receive the word.

A worship song filled Ty'nae's soul with gladness. She loved the praise team at her church. She wasn't much of a singer, but when the spirit moved she sang out loud with glee. She lifted her hands in worship and belted out in her best alto voice. Renee picked up in soprano.

"Our God is greater! Our God is stronger. God you are higher than any other! Our God is healer, awesome in power. Our God, Our God. And if our God be for us then who could ever stop us? And if our God be with us then who can stand against…who can ever stand against?"

Ty'nae sung with all her heart as Renee continued to join in and they both swayed and waved their hands in God's presence. Ty'nae was so grateful that God had met her need. She could go to work without worry. She didn't have to stress over a sitter for Stormy. Yet, she couldn't fully let go of the hurt she felt in her heart over Ryan. She just wanted to know why he left. Although they argued, arguing couldn't have been the main reason because that was something they'd always done from the beginning, but still had stayed together. She couldn't figure out why Ryan would leave his child. Something wasn't right. His inconsistency, abrupt decision making, mood swings and lack of attachment pointed to something deeper. She just didn't know what and God hadn't revealed anything. Ty'nae remembered Renee's words that God had delivered her from Ryan but

Ty'nae couldn't understand why God would let Stormy not have her father. At three months old, Stormy had experienced abandonment. Who would do that to an innocent child? Ty'nae didn't want her daughter to be fatherless. She knew the hurt of that situation all too well herself.

The pastor took the pulpit wearing khaki pants and a white polo shirt. He was short in stature and had a friendly smile. He greeted the congregation and took his text from Proverbs 18:16.

"I want to read this scripture in several different versions on this morning." He said as he put on his glasses.

Ty'nae sat patiently waiting to hear something, anything that could give her hope. She knew what she wanted, so she thought, but she didn't know what she really needed. She didn't know if she should hope for a word concerning Ryan coming home or a word to encourage her to not worry if she never saw him again. Then, her mind went to Stormy, her beautiful three month old bundle of joy. She knew the word she needed was on how to provide as a single mom. Her job paid well, but not well enough to tackle all the bills and a new baby alone in a much larger house than what she was accustomed to handling.

"Does everyone have Proverbs 18:16?" Pastor asked.

You could hear a few replies of, "yes" and "amen" throughout the church.

"Let's read from King James Version first in unison and I will read the other versions aloud to you." He said after clearing his throat.

In unison the congregation read, "A man's gift maketh room for him, and bringeth him before great men."

The pastor went on to quote three other versions of the same scripture.

The first version text stated that a gift opens the way and ushers the giver into the presence of the great. The second was similar, explaining that giving a gift could open doors and it gives access to important people! Lastly, the pastor referred to a version that stated a person's gift makes room for him, and leads him before important people."

Ty'nae and Renee both highlighted the scripture on the back of their church bulletins. They both listened to the pastor attentively.

"My topic today is, 'God show me my gifts!'"

Ty'nae felt disappointed. She felt frustrated. She was hoping he would talk about God providing, relationships being reconciled, hope for the broken hearted. She didn't want to hear about gifts. She wanted her broken heart to find it's healing and feel whole again.

What is this right here? God, I need a word for my situation.

Renee was clueless to her friend's inner thoughts and just smiled, looked at Ty'nae, shrugged her shoulders and continued listening. By the end of the message she'd written four points on her bulletin to remember and so had Ty'nae.

1. We all have been given gifts and talents to share with the world.
2. Those gifts are to aid the body of Christ, but also to assist us in becoming financially empowered.
3. Identify things you enjoy and evaluate if you can use it as a ministry or a business.
4. Ask Holy Spirit to allow you to take that thing which you have identified before people who can make it bigger and better than you ever imagined.

After service, Ty'nae wrote down Renee's address and agreed to drop Stormy off at 7:30 a.m. the next morning. She couldn't thank Renee enough for extending the offer to watch Stormy for free until she could figure things out. If nothing else had come out of her attending church service, she had to at least be grateful that God had met her immediate need.

When Ty'nae entered the nursery, Stormy was bright eyed and making noises as she blew little spit bubbles. One of the high school volunteers working in the nursery quickly came over to introduce herself.

"Hi, I am Lacey. I helped with baby Stormy today."

She told Ty'nae how often Stormy had been changed and fed. Ty'nae thanked her as she took notice of her red spiked hair, nose piercing and tattooed sleeve of gothic images on one arm. At her church, you saw all kinds of people so it didn't bother her at all. Ty'nae grabbed Stormy's diaper bag and took out a light weight, blanket to wrap Stormy in. Once she got to her black Toyota Camry she felt winded. She hurriedly put Stormy into the car seat and by then she was having a hard time catching her breath. She got in the car locked the door and quickly reached for the glove department to retrieve an Albuterol inhaler. She took two puffs and sat as still as she could. It had been a long time since her asthma had bothered her. This was another reason she didn't need to start back smoking. She sat in the car for a while watching other vehicles pull off the lot when out of the corner of her eye she saw a figure approaching the car. She looked out of the window just as a short, stocky, white man got in full sight. She rolled her window down as she recognized him as one of the parking lot attendants who helped out regularly around the church.

"Is everything okay ma'am?" He asked with a concerned look on his face.

"Yes sir…" said Ty'nae as she put the inhaler in the tray underneath her cd player. "…I was just about to leave."

"Not sure how far you are planning to go with that tire nearly flat." He said as he pointed to the back wheel on the driver's side that Ty'nae hadn't even noticed.

"Are you serious?" Ty'nae motioned for the man to step back so she could open the car door. She looked behind her and anger rose up inside of her. It was really low and even though a gas station was right across the street it looked as if she may need it changed not just filled with air.

"Do you have a spare ma'am?" The attendant asked.

"Yes, but I don't know how to change a flat." Ty'nae said frustrated.

"Well my flat fixing days are over but let me go inside the church and find someone to help you." said the old man.

The attendant walked away and Ty'nae could feel anxiety taking over. Again, she felt winded and this time her chest was tight. She needed to sit still inside the car until help arrived. She began to pray to God to calm her nerves and help her not to break down. It felt like she was catching hell all around her and even though one thing had worked out, now she had another thing to deal with. All she wanted was to go home.

Within ten minutes the short, stocky man had returned with a 6'1, dark chocolate, bald headed man behind him. The black man had on dark jeans, a white dress shirt and a very nice looking red tie. He wore some black leather shoes that looked nothing short of expensive. Ty'nae estimated that the man weighed at least 245-250 pounds. She hadn't seen eye candy of his type in a while. Her eyes were excited and her flesh peaked with interest. When they got to the car, the short, stocky man introduced the black man as Brother Seth.

"Hello, Brother Seth. I'm Ty'nae." she extended her hand through the window.

"Nice to meet you." He replied with so much bass in his voice that Ty'nae could feel it in her chest as he spoke.

Now that Brother Seth was in closer view, Ty'nae recalled seeing him play the drums at an earlier service she had attended before. He had also led a solo that day and she could remember how much she enjoyed his singing.

"By the way, I am Brother Thomas." The short, stocky one extended his hand as well.

"I have to go because I pick my grandson up around this time on Sundays, but I'm sure you will be in good care with Brother Seth here." the old man smiled, turned to pat Brother Seth on the shoulder and walked away.

"Well, can we get the spare out of the trunk?" Brother Seth said just as a loud squeal came from the back seat followed by little kicking feet and tears.

"I'm sorry just a moment." Ty'nae said as she turned around to unstrap Stormy from the car seat. She knew that was the cry of hunger.
"O' somebody is unhappy about being out here in the car." Seth said.
"Why don't you take her inside? I will come to get you when I'm done."

Although Ty'nae was not feeling comfortable leaving her keys with a stranger she had no choice. Brother Seth wouldn't get too far in a stolen vehicle that had a flat and she doubted if anyone from the church would steal her car right off the parking lot, but still she hesitated leaving him the car keys.

"Well okay." She said as she got out of the car, handed him the keys and tried to bounce baby Stormy a little to calm her down. She grabbed the diaper bag and as she started to walk away she heard the trunk of her car pop open. She looked back briefly and saw Brother Seth coming from behind the back of the car undoing his red tie. He tossed it through the open window on the driver's side of her car. She felt somewhat of a heatwave go across her face and she tried to keep walking forward without doing a double take but before she could take three steps forward, she looked back once more to see the front of his shirt unbutton and he was about to remove it.

Lord Jesus!

   She picked up the pace and made her way inside the church lobby. By then Stormy had stopped crying and was pulling on one side of Ty'nae's black sweater. Soon as she made it inside the church, Ty'nae stood in the door watching Brother Seth now in a short sleeve all white t-shirt rolling the spare tire around to the side of the car. He threw it down and came back around with a jack and begin lifting the car up. Ty'nae smiled. She was turned on. Brother Seth was fine.

Ump! Ump! Ump!

   Ty'nae found it hard to pry herself away from the glass door but she needed to change and feed Stormy. She went to the ladies room to use the changing table. She kissed all over Stormy as she smiled up at her. Stormy's eyes were so beautiful. Ty'nae felt blessed to have a healthy baby girl. Ryan had done one good thing, Stormy was it, and Ty'nae was so happy to be her mother. She started singing, 'Jesus loves all the little children' to her baby girl. Once she was done she sat out in the hallway near the entrance closer to her car and pulled out a bottle. She put it up to Stormy's mouth as she watched Brother Seth finish up.

She watched him close the trunk and wipe his hands on the front of his jeans. He started walking towards the building with her keys in his hands. Ty'nae perused Seth from head to toe. She liked his skin color, his eyes, and his lips were simply edible looking. She liked his walk and how his jeans fit him. Seth was slightly bow-legged and plain sexy. He smiled as he entered the church and Ty'nae felt moist between the legs. No matter how much she loved the Lord, she was all woman and her flesh craved some physical affection from a man.

"What a heartbreaker…" Seth said as he looked down at Stormy. He'd never seen a baby with that much hair on her head. He wanted to touch it, but didn't think that would be respectful. Stormy looked at him and her little hands reached out to him. He extended his finger and she grabbed it, but let it go quickly.

"Here are your keys. You're good to go whenever she's done with her bottled Big Mac." He laughed and Ty'nae smiled.

Fine and humorous!

"Thanks so much. What do I owe you?" Ty'nae used one hand to try to dig in the cluttered diaper bag for her wallet.

"No, no, no. None of that is necessary. Just be safe. Don't drive on that spare too long." He said and extended his hand.

Ty'nae shook Brother Seth's hand and it felt strong. She took notice of the muscles up and down his chocolate arm and the fact that he was not wearing a wedding band.

"Thank you so very much." She said as she finally released his hand.

"No problem. Take care." Brother Seth walked off and Ty'nae hoped no cameras were recording her as she used her free hand to fan herself.

Well damn! Whew!

Ty'nae was glad no one could read her thoughts as she watched Brother Seth walk away looking like Idris Elba from the back. Ty'nae was thinking all about swerving on top of some black dick. It had been years since she had black dick inside of her. She knew her thoughts weren't right, but she was a work in progress not an overnight wonder, and Jesus himself could see that the man was fine!

Lord, help me get my mind right! Sweet Jesus! He is fine as wine!

3 MIRROR, MIRROR

Ty'nae didn't have a contact number for Brother Seth or Brother Thomas but she wanted to return the red tie and white dress shirt Brother Seth had left in her car. She couldn't believe he had forgotten them. She was sure he was somewhere trying to figure out how to contact her as well. All she could do was make sure she took it back the next Sunday and prayerfully run into him around the church.

She laid Stormy in a colorful baby bouncer and placed the Velcro strap across the front to secure her daughter tightly. She started peeling off her sweater and kicked off her black pumps so she could step out of her dark denim jeans. She stood in the living room with her 'Flawless' t-shirt on and a red thong. She put a side knot in the t-shirt and looked down at her toes. The sight of chipped polish was disappointing. She looked at her finger nails too as they were also void of polish. She walked over to the big mirror on the wall above the couch and ran her hand over her afro that needed some TLC. She really wanted a sew-in style. The mirror didn't lie. She really needed to co-wash her natural hair. The blond color still looked vibrant but she needed a hot oil treatment. It needed to be shaped up as well, since she had an important meeting to conduct. Her boss never complained about her hair. Many of the other African American women she worked with had natural styles and various colors. It seemed it mattered more how you carried yourself than how you expressed your personality through your hair style. She loved the atmosphere at her work. There were a few co-workers with strong racial opinions, but for the most part, the majority were supportive of equal opportunities. She only had an associate's degree, but she was well spoken and computer savvy. Ty'nae also was very confident of her skill set.

Ty'nae decided to spend the rest of her Sunday trying to get her appearance up to part for work. She wanted to look fashionable and professional for her meeting. All eyes would be on her and she wanted to give them an eyeful to stare at. First, she packed a bag for Stormy to take to Renee's and sat it by the door. She knew that would help her save time in the morning and she planned to prepare bottles before bedtime. Then, she took all of her dirty clothes and put them in one pile out of her way. The house was already a mess so to her it didn't matter that she was adding a pile of clothes to the mix. At least now, she was responsible for cleaning up her own mess and not Ryan's. He always left a trail through the house.

She went to the kitchen and grabbed a shiny red apple from the fruit bowl. She washed it, wrapped it in a paper towel and came back to the living room to crawl up on the couch. Her house was always filled with plenty of fruits and vegetables because healthy eating was something Ryan insisted on and she had soon learned to comply. Actually, she appreciated him for his outlook on health because even though she had a nice shape when they met, she had dropped ten more pounds and gotten toned. She also felt better now that she wasn't filling her body with sugar and processed foods all the time. She knew that her healthy eating habits contributed to her problem free pregnancy.

Ty'nae pulled Stormy's bouncer a little closer to her and reached for the remote control to the black, RCA, flat screen television. The house was quiet and she battled thoughts of Ryan. It wasn't that she missed him it was that she didn't understand why he had left or where he could possibly be. She didn't want to call his parents; they weren't that supportive of their relationship from the beginning. He'd never brought anyone around accept for Sam. She didn't really have a clue as to who else he could be staying with. Sam was the only friend he had as far as Ty'nae had known. Ryan and Sam seemed to spend time after work frequently. They never hung out at the house, just went to happy hour together and occasionally Ryan would say he was playing video games at Sam's house. Sam allowed Ryan to keep the cars he got for his future car lot stored at his family's farm. Sam was single and very athletic; always running marathons. He was the only cowboy type Ty'nae had ever met personally. He was also a dog owner and on a few occasions, Ryan had doggy sat for him when he needed to go out of town. There was no one else Ty'nae could imagine Ryan would be with unless he had gotten a hotel or apartment somewhere. However, what she wasn't going to do was waste time looking for and chasing after any man that had the audacity to leave his own child. Ty'nae began to think about their joint finances. She hoped Ryan wouldn't take all of their money. She used her cell phone and with the mobile app for online banking she pulled up their mutual account and saw no activity over the last few days. There wasn't much money there, but at least it didn't show that he had withdrawn anything. That gave her heart ease. She needed the Lord to help her to stop obsessing over the whole situation.

Ty'nae used her foot to rock the bouncer as Stormy cooed away and seemed to enjoy her fist in her mouth. Ty'nae took a big bite of her apple, placed it on the coffee table and left to go get nail polish remover, cotton balls and her favorite Senorita Rose-alita nail polish by OPI. She sat back on the couch talking baby talk to Stormy and watching television as she focused on her feet first. When they were done she prompted them on the coffee table to dry.

Soon Stormy fell off to sleep in the bouncer and the house felt so much lonelier. Ty'nae tried to not let it get to her. She started on her finger nails and when they were done she carefully tried to change the channel with the remote control and happened upon a program about women entrepreneurs. Ty'nae was proud of Renee stepping out on faith to start her daycare. She had thought about opening some sort of business more than once or twice but she never really seriously attempted to follow through with a plan. She was interested in the segment. She wondered how she could make some money on the side. Her job wouldn't be enough for all the bills and Stormy's needs. Even though Renee wasn't charging her for childcare, she didn't want to burden her and was trying to figure out in her mind how much she could afford for permanent childcare.

It seemed like each woman on the television show she was watching had started their business out of desperation to make extra money. Many of them had turned their hobbies into ways to make easy money. Ty'nae thought back to the morning's sermon and found a connection with the television show. She waited for her nails to dry completely and then went to retrieve the church bulletin she had took notes on during service. She re-read the notes and pondered if God was speaking to her after all.

1. We all have been given gifts and talents to share with the world.

2. Those gifts are to aid the body of Christ, but also to assist us in becoming financially empowered.

3. Identify things you enjoy and evaluate if you can use it as a ministry or a business.

4. Ask Holy Spirit to allow you to take that thing which you have identified before people who can make it bigger and better than you ever imagined.

She prayed silently that God would show her what gifts she had that she could use to make money. Many of her hobbies had been on hold. For the life of her, she couldn't come up with a reason why she had allowed being in a relationship with Ryan to consume so much of her. When she lived in Memphis, she used to love painting and sewing. She wasn't the best painter but she had worked her way into doing nature scenes pretty well. She knew she could sell her paintings. Sewing was a skill she learned from her grandmother. Skirts were the easiest for her and she loved to make dresses. She made a few handkerchiefs for the ladies at her grandmothers' church in the past. She'd even made pillows to donate to special charities that her grandmother was involved in back home. Sewing was time consuming. She didn't have a lot of time for cutting patterns and sewing, not with a new born baby and a full time job. Yet, she believed God would show her what she could do to make money. If Ryan ever came back, she wouldn't take him and if he didn't contact her soon, she'd have to seek assistance through the state to afford formula, childcare and etc. If Ryan wanted out that was fine but he still needed to financially support his child. He needed to be a part of his baby girl's life. Just thinking about him made Ty'nae so angry. She knew she had to come up with a plan on the side to financially be okay no matter what happened concerning Ryan. Stormy was *her* baby and she had to provide.

The television show went off and Ty'nae tucked her notes from service in the night stand drawer next to her bed. She went back to the living room to get Stormy and placed her baby in the crib for the night; she hoped. She took all the dishes out of the sink and stacked them on the counter. She started to co-wash her hair in the kitchen sink and afterwards ironed work clothes for the week. Lastly, she drew herself a bubble bath and added some lavender Epsom salt to soothe her tired body. While in the tub, she sipped on a glass of white wine. Her mind tried to race all over the place but she prayed for peace.

When she was done bathing, she gently dried her body with a soft white towel. She wondered if she should put a leave in conditioner on her hair and sleep in her stocking cap and satin bonnet. It always made her hair a little more manageable as the curls wouldn't be as tight and much easier to pick out. She squirted a little leave in conditioner in her hand, rubbed it through and put the stocking cap on. She looked in the mirror remembering how she used to look before going all natural. She went to the bathroom closet and took out an old wig and placed it on her head just for something to do. The stocking cap was snug enough that the wig didn't look puffy. She found a comb and started to comb the tangles out of it. The wig was similar to how she used to wear her hair and every blue moon if bored; she would wear the wig and switch up her look for a day or two. She was determined to find enough money for the sew in she longed for because she really desired to have a softer more curly look. She stood in the mirror butt naked just looking at the wig, her face, and her beautiful breast. She started to wonder about another night without sex. It all wasn't fair. Ryan and she had a great sex life if nothing else. No matter how she wanted to get him off her mind the fact was that his absence was causing her several issues.

Ty'nae went to the living room and pushed the button on the CD player. She turned it down so it wouldn't wake Stormy and she tried to dance around in the long wig to the sounds of Beyoncé's song, *'Partition'*. She was doing nothing more but wasting time. Going to bed alone wasn't something she was looking forward to.

Ty'nae noticed the white shirt and red tie she'd brought in from her car. She thought all about that dark, chocolate, fine Brother Seth. She slipped the white shirt onto her naked body. It was way too big but felt good on her bare flesh. She took the tie and put it on her neck and rolled the sleeves of the shirt up midway her arm. Ty'nae took a sip of wine, grabbed a chair from the kitchen and put the Beyoncé song on replay. She danced to *'Partition'* all around the chair then sat in it with her legs crossed. She started to pretend she was dancing for Brother Seth. She put the tie between her teeth around her neck and then stood up with one foot in the chair and stroked the tie between her legs. She thought about how she would handcuff him with the tie if he was there. Then, her jam came on and Ty'nae got loose with it. That big booty of hers was putting in work. She was smiling and feeling sexy.

Yoncé' all on his mouth like liquor
like, like liquor, like, like, like liquor
Yoncé' all on his mouth like liquor
like, like liquor, like, like, like liqour

Ty'nae had moves. She laughed at herself. She knew she needed to quit but she was every bit human. Plus, she really felt no one knew her as well as God and she honestly didn't think he was overly concerned with her playing around when there were bigger things going on in the world for him to focus attention on, like starving children and cancer patients. Problems of daily living were more important than his silly daughter dancing to Beyoncé. Ty'nae shook her big booty and tried to see herself in the mirror above the couch but it wasn't positioned low enough for her to take it all in. She was proud of her body and wanted to look at it as she moved to the music. She went in her bedroom and slowly pushed her wardrobe mirror to the living room. It was tall and on a wooden stand but it wasn't heavy. She just didn't want to wake Stormy, so she took her time.

Ty'nae positioned the mirror just right and she danced in that white shirt and red tie through every single song on the surprise creative work Beyoncé had released at the end of 2013. It was eight months later and Ty'nae was still wearing the CD out! Dancing made her feel good. Dancing made her feel sexy. Dancing took the pain away for a little while. She wasn't even thinking about Brother Seth inappropriately anymore, she was just dancing and enjoying the fact that pregnancy hadn't destroyed her sexy shape. She noticed a long piece of red thread hanging from Brother Seth's tie. She felt so bad and knew she was to blame. She tried to wrap the thread around her finger and break it off but it only made matters worse as more thread began to unravel. She felt so guilty that she had obviously messed up his tie. She also knew with the way she'd been sweating, she needed to put his shirt in the cleaners. Ty'nae tried to find a needle and red thread so she could repair the tie. As she examined the tie she looked at how it was put together. The fabric felt good in her hand but she questioned the quality of the work. With a seamstress eye, she evaluated how the fabric could have been secured better. She repaired the tie and it looked pretty good but she still felt that wasn't enough for having made the tie come undone in the first place. Ty'nae wondered how easy it would be to make a tie. She'd never tried but she figured if she could make a skirt, a dress, handkerchiefs and pillows then surely a tie couldn't be too much of a challenge.

Ty'nae yanked the wig that had now become annoying off of her head and threw it on the couch. She went to get her satin bonnet and placed it on top of the stocking cap already on her head. She found a pair of boy shorts to cover her plump behind and a tank to pull over her perky breast. She peeked in on the baby and found her still resting peaceful. Ty'nae, looked through her closet for something she hadn't worn in a long time that she wouldn't mind cutting. She searched and searched through her fashion clutter and decided on a blue, cotton shirt with a stripped pattern on it. She grabbed a pair of sewing scissors from a box she kept buried in the back of her closet. She went to sit on the couch with the fabric in her hand and held Brother Seth's tie up and compared its length to the fabric. She took a better look at the back of his tie and how the seams where put together. Without a pattern or a measuring tape, Ty'nae cut her shirt up just perfectly. Correct length, width, shape…she knew grandma would be ever so proud. She went to the kitchen and plugged up her iron. She starched the fabric and folded it perfectly in the way she wanted it and then ironed the creases in place. Then, she found thread to match the fabric and by hand begin to enclose a perfect seam. She wasn't ready to start with a sewing machine as of yet, but practicing by hand helped her to see exactly how to secure the seam so that the thread wouldn't fall apart. When she was done, she stood in front of her wardrobe mirror and tied the tie around her neck better than any man. It was perfect! She liked it so much she decided she'd wear it to work. The mirror didn't lie. In its reflective light, Ty'nae had found her gift.

4 WALK ON WATER

Ty'nae overslept by fifteen minutes. Being up all night playing around with one piece of fabric after the other was now causing her to yawn over and over again. She had created twelve ties before she'd finally fell off to sleep. She made bright ones, dark ones, cotton and silk ones, and a quirky one for those who enjoyed dressing in nerd fashion. She made some for ladies and others for gentlemen. She was up to her neck in ties. True to her obsessive personality she couldn't stop once she started. Her mind had got to racing and before long she had grabbed a notebook and wrote the name of her new business, 'All Tied Up', at the top of a piece of paper. Underneath, she wrote her mission statement, a lengthy supply list and decided to begin selling them for $10.00. Ever the one with a given heart, Ty'nae had decided to donate ten percent of her tie sales to Kappa League to help the boys in the organization with their college tour trips. She also wrote a goal to make ties to donate to the League so that boys that didn't have ties for special events could benefit from her business.

She was sleepy, but full of adrenaline because she felt hopeful that she could pull a small business of this sort off easily. She got Stormy ready to go to Renee's home daycare and she put her in the bouncer for long enough for her to throw herself together. Her hair was so soft from the leave in conditioner she'd put in it the night before. Ty'nae put on some cover girl bronzer, black eyeliner and iridescent lip gloss. She opted for large silver hoop earrings with a matching silver ring and bracelet. She wore a white, button down, business shirt and the very first tie she made. It was a blue, cotton tie with strips in dark navy, gray and red. She had on a dark blue suit jacket with a fitted blue skirt that made her booty look absolutely fabulous. She took her snazzy outfit even further when she put on a pair of Anne Klein red pumps and grabbed a small red clutch to match. She put just a dot of coconut oil in her hand and spread it throughout her fro and fingered it instead of picking it out. She washed off her hands, dried them and just stood admiring herself in the bathroom mirror.

Hair done, nails done, everything done!

Her hair looked so fly that all Ty'nae could do was smile. She made sure all her notes for the meeting where inside of her Coach portfolio and she grabbed Stormy and was out the door in a flash.

Renee was standing in the door looking out when Ty'nae pulled up at 7:50 a.m., twenty minutes later than planned and she looked worried. Ty'nae was certain that Renee thought she had gotten lost in her subdivision which was a little tricky with how the street numbers ran. But it was her late night spent making ties that had her running so late on a Monday morning. Renee got the diaper bag and unbuckled Stormy from the car seat and walked up the cobblestone path to Renee's front door.

"You look gooooood girl! Give me that tie!" Renee said talking way too loud early in the morning. She put a hand on her hip and smiled brightly.

"Thanks sis, I made it!" Ty'nae smiled with pride as she motioned to put Stormy into Renee's arms and waited a second for Renee to open them for the baby. Ty'nae sat the diaper bag right inside the door of the house.

"Get out of here! I didn't know you make ties!" Renee looked surprised.

"Me neither, I just made it and a few more last night." She said excitedly as she was very proud of her creation.

"You got talent ma'am! It's hot! That tie and them heels sets the entire outfit off! You better work it!"

Ty'nae smiled. She knew if Renee was complimenting her it was sincere. She also knew that when it came to fashion, Renee didn't short step so if she said the tie was hot it really was.

"I wanted to get here on time and take a look around but I really need to get to work because my meeting starts at 8:15. I'm really pushing it." She hugged Renee and kissed Stormy on the forehead and started to walk towards the car.

"I understand. She is in good care. Don't worry. Have a blessed day at work." Renee said as she watched Ty'nae get into the black Camry and back out of the drive way in a hurry.

Ty'nae got about two blocks away from Renee's house and anxiety crept in. She started to feel like she wasn't a good mother because she hadn't gotten any references on Renee. She hadn't even gone inside of the house to ensure it was clean and safe. She started to wonder if leaving her baby girl was the best idea. It's not that she had any other choices but she kept thinking maybe she was being way too trusting of a woman she only knew through church. The clock was ticking and instead of letting the devil drive her crazy, Ty'nae started to have a talk with God in the car.

"Lord, I need you. I am feeling so much anxiety right now. I believe that Renee is your child and I want to be okay with this whole childcare thing, but I am struggling. I could pinch myself for running late this morning because now my child is there and I haven't even seen the inside of Renee's house. Can you please cover Stormy in your blood? Can you please dispatch your angels all around my sweet baby Heavenly Father? Please help me to get through this meeting dear God and Lord, where ever Ryan is right now can you please talk to his heart about me and Stormy. I really need you to talk to his heart about us." By the time she finished tears were running down her face and she was trying to pull herself together. Her make-up was too cute to ruin. She knew she wouldn't have time to check herself in the ladies room once she got to work. She needed to go straight to the conference room and prayed that someone had already started brewing coffee.

She arrived with not even five minutes to spare. Ty'nae walked into the room wearing a smile and went straight over to the coffee area for some decaf. She then, walked over to the conference table to greet her boss and three other department heads. Susan entered in with a smile.

"Glad you are here, Ty'nae! I was thinking about you all the way to work. Wasn't sure you had a sitter." Susan said.

"Yes, it worked out. A lady from church has Stormy today." Her voice sounded relieved.

"Great! Nice tie, by the way. Very attractive. Break a leg this morning. Don't let these mean faces intimidate you." Susan spoke from experience as she had been in Ty'nae's shoes before and knew leading the Monday meetings were brutal.

Ty'nae had held a supervisor position in the IT department of a big name metal supply company in the area since moving to St. Louis. In Memphis, she had done the same work for a similar company that diversified its metals and supplied related equipment. She had moved to St. Louis to pursue her current position because of this company's vision to expand its marketplace by extending services to machine shops, healthcare facilities, universities and untapped government agencies throughout the St. Louis region. The company was already filling orders in several states and by tapping into local government they would be prepared to start up other companies in cities that had government agencies that needed servicing. The job had room for growth and the pay was decent. Now in her situation as a single mom, she needed to do everything she could to move up in the company and make some side money. She couldn't think about Ryan at the time but he was always lurking in the back of her mind, almost taunting her with worries of how she would provide for Stormy without him.

"Nice tie! Very tasteful! " Her boss said as she handed her a copy of the data charts she'd requested previously.

"Thank you, Mrs. Rizzle. I made it myself." Ty'nae smiled.

"Really? Well, aren't you full of surprise talent?" Mrs. Rizzle said as she looked the tie over once more and admired how Ty'nae had really put together a nice appearance for today's meeting.

"I appreciate the compliment, Mrs. Rizzle." Ty'nae said as she passed out copies of the agenda to everyone present and placed an electronic copy of the data chart up on the promethean board for everyone to see. The hard copy she had in her hand was so she could refer to it as she spoke to the staff. She opened the meeting full of confidence, a bright smile and a tie that was everything!

It was an hour and fifteen minutes when the meeting was adjourned and it seemed like everyone wanted to come up to her not just to compliment her on conducting a professional meeting but to inquire about her tie. Most of them couldn't get over the fact that she had made it herself. Ty'nae was glad she had eleven more already made because if the one she was wearing was getting so much attention she couldn't wait to hear input about the others.

The work day dragged on and Ty'nae was drinking coffee every hour on the hour to stay awake. She called Renee on her lunch break to check on Stormy. Renee assured her that Stormy was fine and that she had already had a feeding and two diaper changes. Ty'nae couldn't wait to get to her baby. She didn't know if she could get use to someone other than her and Ryan caring for Stormy. She kept being prayerful throughout the day. She now understood what her grandmother use to say about asking Jesus to be a fence all around you. She had been praying a fence around Stormy all day.

Handling Business

When the day ended at 4:30 p.m. Ty'nae rushed to get to Stormy. She knocked on the door and it seemed to take five minutes or more for Renee to answer which made her very nervous. When Renee got to the door she explained that her niece had just knocked over a big container of cheese puffs and when she started toward the door she realized crushed orange cheese puffs from the bottom of her shoe was leaving marks in the carpet so she back tracked to the kitchen to kick them off before coming to the door.

Ty'nae walked in and looked around. The environment was very homey. Renee really knew how to put a house together. Everything was so expensive looking and Ty'nae loved all the scripture based artwork that occupied the walls. Deep burgundy, olive green and gold was consistent throughout every room she passed on her way to the kitchen. A faint smell of rose petal sweet oil burned on a lamp burner and lightly permeated throughout the house. Ty'nae also inhaled a pleasant scent coming from the kitchen and as she walked behind Renee, she could see two crock pots going on the counter. There was a pan of fresh baked cornbread sitting on top of the stove. Renee grabbed the broom and looked back to tell Ty'nae to watch her step. She swept all the corn puffs into a pile. Ty'nae saw the empty cheese puff container sitting on the table. She had purchased one of those big tubs before herself from the local Dollar General Store. Renee told her niece to help in a very stern voice.

"Come on Mookie, you can at least hold the trash bag!"

The two year old girl with slanted eyes and five barrettes in her curly hair got up from the chair and went to hold the trash bag while Renee poured the contents from the dust pan into it. It took 3 dumps before the floor was cleaned up. Ty'nae could tell that Mookie was spoiled. Whoever had dressed her made sure that her little nail polish matched her outfit. Every barrette was strategically placed. Her outfit was so adorable as if right out of a *Carters* clothing catalog.

Ty'nae waited for the mess to all be up before she crossed the floor to get to Stormy who was lying peacefully asleep in a bassinet that rocked back and forth if you winded it up. She seemed to be just fine.

"Now, go sit back at the table Mookie and color until I get some butter on this cornbread." Renee said as she multitasked around the kitchen.

"How was work?" She finally managed to ask Ty'nae who was still admiring Stormy peacefully asleep.

"It went well. I really appreciate you for watching Stormy."

"No problem..." she said as she smoothed butter on top of the warm cornbread and then searched for two containers.

"You sure got it smelling good up in here! What are you cooking?" Ty'nae asked trying not to overly salivate.

"Well Ms. Lady, this right here is your dinner!" She turned around and gave Ty'nae a playful wink and a smile.

"What? Girl, no you didn't cook for me." Ty'nae had a look of disbelief on her face.

"O' yes I did! You are going to be glad I did too." Renee showed her pearly whites and then looked over at the table to see Mookie fidgeting.

"Go potty girl! Right this second!" Renee said to Mookie.

The little girl got out of the chair, put her thumb in her mouth, rolled her eyes and went to the bathroom off the side of the kitchen. She kept the door wide open as she lifted up the lid of a potty, pulled her pants and pull up down simultaneously and sat on the potty.

"Wow, she is pretty young for potty training isn't she?" Ty'nae inquired.

"Maybe, but I won't be changing no diapers on her big butt, so I told my sister she was going to learn how to potty over here!" Renee went over to the bathroom door and pulled it up just a little so that Mookie could have her privacy.

"Okay, I'm almost done packing you up so why don't you get Stormy together and head out to the car and I will be right behind you with your dinner." Renee was moving at a fast pace and even with a lot to do she did it looking fabulous.

Renee had a little red flower on the side of her hair. The Malaysian weave made her look like she was from the Islands. She had on a cute red, dainty see thru top and a red camisole tank up under it. Renee had on some white shorts and cute red and gold sandals. She had a gold ankle bracelet on and an arm full of red and white bangles that made lots of noise as she hurried back and forth.

Ty'nae had Stormy all ready and just as Renee had requested, she headed to the car. Renee went into the bathroom to help Mookie and the next thing Ty'nae knew Renee had a big bag in one hand and was holding Mookie's hand with the other. Mookie was also carrying a small, lightweight bag.

Everything was placed on the floor of the front seat and hugs were exchanged then Ty'nae was headed for home.

The drive home was peaceful as Stormy did not make a wink. Ty'nae kept looking in her rearview mirror at Stormy every time the car came to a stop light just to make sure she looked okay.

No sooner as they arrived home, Ty'nae kicked off her heels and peeled herself out of the suit jacket that was making her hot. Ty'nae tried to figure out why Stormy was crying all of a sudden. She screamed to the top of her lungs and kicked her little feet until both socks came off. Ty'nae unzipped her skirt and left it on the floor where she stepped out of it at and finally undid her tie and shirt leaving her in a pair of sheer skin tone stockings, white panties with the garter buttons and a sexy, white lace bra that Ryan had bought her from a Pure Romance catalog. Ty'nae prepared a bottle and it seemed as if that calmed Stormy down. After her feeding, Stormy got changed and put down in bed. Ty'nae went to the kitchen made a glass of ice tea and prepared to eat. She reached into the heavy bag and pulled out two containers. One had shrimp gumbo in it and the other had homemade chicken soup with vegetables and rice in it. Ty'nae opted for the gumbo so she retrieved a bowl from the cabinet and poured herself a nice portion. She went into the smaller bag and pulled out two hunks of aluminum foil. One had buttered cornbread and the other was a piece of pound cake. Ty'nae felt blessed. The gumbo was delicious just like the kind she'd eaten when she visited Louisiana one summer. The shrimp were so large and it was seasoned to perfection. She enjoyed every bite of her meal. She appreciated the sisterhood between her and Renee.

When she was done, she put the left over contents in the refrigerator but talked herself out of cleaning her dishes. Instead she went over to the couch and picked up some fabric, turned on the television and started making new tie creations. She picked up the notebook nearby and each time a thought came to her she'd jot it down...website, business cards, PayPal account, online boutiques to self-manage, register a 'doing business as' form, open a business account, check community college for business tax class, create flyers, promote product, get labels, order boxes to distribute ties in, talk to beauty and barber shop owners, find places to display my product...the list went on and on. Before the night was over, Ty'nae had made seventeen ties by hand! She'd stopped here and there to see after Stormy but every time Stormy went to sleep, Ty'nae worked harder.

She was tired but something kept pushing her, driving her and she felt inspired. She didn't want to sleep she just wanted to keep working on her new business venture. She knew it would take strong faith to pull this venture off. She reminded herself about a bible story she had read about one of Christ disciples named Peter who wanted to walk on water. Jesus told him to come and as long as he stayed focused on Christ he stayed on the water with no problem. It was only when he took his eyes off of Jesus that he began to doubt and could no longer walk on the water. Ty'nae determined in her heart in that moment that she would be the one that kept the faith she would be the one to fix her eyes on Jesus and the gift he'd revealed to her. She was starting her own business, 'All Tied Up' and with

God's help she would walk on water!

5 HOPE WILL HEAL

Weeks had passed and July had arrived with its sweltering heat. Ty'nae had finally started to adjust to life without Ryan. She had to confess that between church and Renee she had no choice but to keep fighting because all her encouragement came from them. Ty'nae was still trying to work her way up at her day job and her evening and weekend gig making ties was bringing in an extra $300 bucks a month. She had bought a new tire for her car and was making plans to pay off her credit cards one at a time. She had extended her craft to include bow ties as well. God had opened doors for her quickly.

The following Sunday after meeting Brother Seth she had returned his items to him and included several of her handmade ties as a gift. It was her way to apologize for damaging his tie. Little did she know that he would share with the other brothers around church how nice the ties she made look.

The youth praise band had ordered ties. The deacon's board had ordered ties. And all the ministers in the church were supporting her business, 'All Tied Up' as well. Ladies from church were ordering ties for the men in their lives. Ty'nae was getting new orders every Sunday and the more she made the better she got at it. She had even learned how to sew a little label inside of the back of the tie that had an imprint of her company's name, "All Tied Up". She was passing out business cards everywhere she went and not only were her ties appealing to men but some women started catching the tie fever too. It was sexy for a woman to sport a tie with her outfit. It made a bold statement. Her boss, Mrs. Rizzle had purchased several of Ty'nae's tie creations and the people in the office found it to be the new rave.

Renee was a true fan of Ty'nae's ties also. She not only purchased a few but arranged to have a party at her house to introduce Ty'nae's new line of ties to her family and friends. She helped Ty'nae come up with a jazzy logo for the business and as a gift she invested $500.00 into Ty'nae's new business venture so that she could go to the fabric store for materials. Renee was truly a friend sent from God. She cheered for Ty'nae every step of the way. It seemed the more Renee poured into Ty'nae's life the more God was blessing Renee's daycare and more children were starting to attend.

Ty'nae had sat down and looked over her budget and it looked as if she could pay Renee' at least $65.00 a week for taking care of Stormy, but

Renee would not accept it. She told Ty'nae that she would continue to watch the baby for free until January. That way, Ty'nae could catch up on bills, grow her business and have a solid financial plan to stabilize things for her and her child.

With all the positive things going on in Ty'nae's life she wasn't craving cigarettes at all. As time aided in healing her wounds she was spending time in God's word daily, growing in her faith and sleeping in her bed wasn't as hard as when Ryan first left. She'd gotten enough motivation to clean her house top to bottom and as she did she packed up everything that Ryan had left behind to set out for the trash man to pick up. She also got rid of the awful toss pillows in the living room and with the help of Renee she had repainted the accent wall to match the other walls in the kitchen. The place was starting to look like her house. She also had contacted the landlord and explained the situation. It was so humiliating to talk about being walked out on by the father of her child. The landlord was understanding and re-did all the paperwork in Ty'nae's name. Since the landlord was also a woman that had been through some personal challenges as well, she felt compassion for Ty'nae. She lowered the rent on the house by fifty bucks! Ty'nae was now using that extra money towards her utilities. Things were working out in Ty'nae's favor. God was meeting every need and she was no longer walking in fear of single motherhood. Her baby was getting big and it was amazing to see her developing. She was the sunshine in Ty'nae's life. She also liked how Stormy was becoming very comfortable with Renee as her caregiver. God had hooked it all up just right and Ty'nae gave Him all the glory.

Every Sunday Brother Seth would make his way over to Ty'nae's side of the sanctuary to say hello to her and Stormy. Renee had started to tease Ty'nae as she was always labeling Brother Seth as Ty'nae's *boo-thang*. She was full of jokes, but Ty'nae did like Brother Seth. His eyes were kind, his smile genuine and he always asked if there was anything she needed done. Several times, Ty'nae felt so proud of how he matched up her hand made ties with his attire. One Sunday, he asked if he could have her phone number and mentioned he would really like to get to know her outside of First Christian Church. Their phone conversations pretty much focused on the same themes such as God, family and her new business. Soon, Brother Seth asked Ty'nae out on a date. She was so happy for the invite but it made her start thinking about being jilted by Ryan again. She didn't want to get herself all excited just to be let down. Plus, she didn't want to start seeing someone and they not be considerate of Stormy who'd just turned five months. Renee thought it was a great idea. She'd been secretly praying about the situation. She noticed how Seth looked at Ty'nae and how he was always buying ties and wearing them to help promote, All Tied Up. She could tell that Seth was on a search for a wife. Renee assured her friend that she would watch the baby while she went out for a good time. She believed God was moving in Ty'nae's life in a special way.

So on a warm night in July, Ty'nae put on a cute white sundress with a pair of turquoise stone earrings she'd purchased from an on-line jewelry boutique called Annie Mae's along with a necklace that matched. She put on some cute white sandals that had little summer charms that came up the front of the shoe and then wrapped around the ankle and fastened with a gold hook. The look was comfortable and fashionable for summer time. Seth had mentioned that the place they were going to was like a sports bar but on this particular night people didn't really dress up to hang out there. He also mentioned not to wear heels because he loved the band performing and would want to dance most of the night. Ty'nae's afro had grown out a lot so she pulled it up on one side with a flower since she loved how Renee would put flowers in her hair sometimes. The look still worked even with natural hair and with just a little make up, Ty'nae was ready to go to a Dirty Muggs concert out in West Port Plaza. She dropped Stormy off to Renee who complimented her on her look and encouraged her to have fun with Seth.

Ty'nae didn't know the area well, and had passed up the place more than once but finally realized she was in the correct plaza. She parked her Camry, and walked into the establishment. It was packed. Seth was right, the people weren't dressed up much but everyone seemed friendly. Seth noticed her coming through the door and before she could go any further he walked up to greet her. She felt butterflies in her stomach as she inhaled his Euphoria cologne. Seth hugged her and she thought she'd melt right there in front of everyone. His body was comfortable, his arms felt so strong and his height overshadowing her which made being in his arms feel so secure. He took her hand and led her to the back of the bar where he had already secured a table for the two of them. Ty'nae liked his denim jeans that he wore so well and the simple red polo shirt that lay on his chest perfectly. He was wearing the latest Jordan's and the relaxed look worked for him.

When the waiter arrived at the table, Ty'nae ordered a Sprite with cherries and Seth ordered Vodka with club soda and lime. Both looked over the menu and decided to split an order of loaded french-fries and both got a basket of hot wings with celery sticks. Seth was very humorous and kept cracking jokes and talking about his childhood and college days. Ty'nae laughed until tears came from her eyes as Seth talked about his family. His description of his upbringing was just as funny as the sitcom, 'Everybody hates Chris'. Then, as the conversation went on, Seth dropped the bomb about his criminal past that completely floored Ty'nae. She never would have guessed all he'd been through and she was amazed at how transparent Seth was with her.

Tales of hanging with the wrong people who didn't bother to tell him that they'd stolen a vehicle and robbed a store before picking him up for a party led to talks about time spent in jail and the struggles of being acclimated to society once his time was served. Talks of job training programs, an ex and a thirteen year old kid that lived in Kansas City all seemed pretty much for first date conversation. Ty'nae begin to think that the Vodka Seth had ordered must have been much needed to tell his story. However, Ty'nae felt good that Seth was so comfortable to entrust her with his personal life even if *truth syrup* helped him. In times past, she would have instantly thought of these things as a deal breaker, but for some reason, she was sitting there looking at Seth with wanting eyes and accepting the man he was not someone he could have pretended to be.

And then God's presence sat at the table, and Seth began to share his testimony of how God changed his life, restored his soul and was calling him into ministry. Ty'nae was amazed at how this man just opened up his reality to her and when he was done, he asked if she could see herself dating an imperfect man with a tainted past that was now a born again Christian and planning to live the rest of his life as a minister of the gospel.

It was all too much to digest at once, but Ty'nae thanked him for trusting her with the information he'd provided and told him she was willing to date him to see where things would go.

They finished their meal and went to another room where a pool table and dart game was in plain sight. They spent about thirty minutes in there and soon there was an announcement that the band of the night was hitting the stage in 10, 9, 8…all of a sudden the music was loud, the people hit the center floor in front of the stage and Seth grabbed Ty'nae and pulled her on the floor with him. It had been so long since Ty'nae danced in public even though her private performances were on lock. However, in the safety and comfort of Seth's presence she was feeling herself and the beat of the music crept into her hips and before long her big butt was working it on the floor and Seth liked how she worked it!

They danced together every song and when the band went on break, Seth asked if she was open to a drink.

"Would you like some wine?" He asked reluctantly. He knew that some Christians didn't drink wine and he wasn't trying to offend her or make his own faith seem phony. He was a man that enjoyed sipping sometimes on his nights out. He wasn't an over consumer and had never had any problem behaviors related to drinking.

"Yes, I'd like a glass of Chardonnay." Ty'nae said with a smile. She too wasn't a winebibber but occasionally she liked to sip. There was no history of misuse of alcohol in her past and she really didn't care what other church people thought about her.

They slow danced and sipped and truly had a great time. When the band played their last song the place cleared out. They decided to let the crowd go first and then when only a few stragglers were in the place, Seth walked Ty'nae to her vehicle. They hugged good bye and Ty'nae left to pick up Stormy.

On the drive to Renee's house, Ty'nae couldn't stop singing all the songs the Dirty Muggs had performed and she couldn't wait to tell Renee that their lead singer was sexy! Between the lead singer and Seth, Ty'nae had had all the eye candy a church going girl could stand!

She arrived at Renee's and when she walked in the door Stormy was screaming at the top of her lungs. Ty'nae rushed pass Renee to find Stormy in a pumpkin seat all upset.

"I didn't want to disturb you on your date, but I'm thinking she has an ear infection. She has been pulling on her left ear and screaming to high heaven." Renee said as she watched Ty'nae pick Stormy up and hold her close.

"You should have called! I would have come!" Ty'nae was not happy and her tone expressed it.

Renee threw both hands on her hips and looked Ty'nae in the eye shocked at the tone she was using towards her. "Well, I gave her some Motrin because she had a little fever. Before I gave it to her, I called Children's Hospital hotline. I wrote everything they said on a note pad for you along with the number. They recommended getting her in to see a pediatrician as soon as possible and to administer the Motrin every four hours until the fever stays gone for 24 hours."

"Thanks Renee." Ty'nae said. She looked Stormy over and she seemed fine, but obviously irritated.

"So how was your hot date?" Renee inquired as she was not about to trip over Ty'nae's overly protective self. She was all anxious to hear the news.

"It went well. Thanks so much for watching the baby for me."

"You are welcome. Hey, listen, I could have called you, but you needed this night" She touched her friends shoulder gently. She knew that God had assigned her to be a blessing to Ty'nae and Stormy. She refused to let the devil bring in a little fox to destroy their friendship.

"I knew that Stormy would be okay. I apologize for upsetting you by not calling but the operator on the hotline assured me that Motrin was the only thing that could help until you got her checked out. These ear infections can be rough on little ones." Renee said, hoping that Ty'nae wouldn't second guess her childcare ability and see that her heart was tender towards her and Stormy.

Ty'nae knew that Renee had both her and Stormy's best interest at heart. She hugged her friend and apologized to her.

"So tell me sis, how was it?" Renee egged Ty'nae to spill the beans.

"Well, Brother Seth is sexy and I found out tonight he is a little rough around the edges too." Ty'nae laughed. Renee put her hands on her hips, "Aint nothing like a bad boy to a good girl hunty!" She laughed playfully and the two of them kept smiling.

Ty'nae told Renee all about his past and how he'd shared a powerful testimony about how God had saved him and was now calling him into the ministry.

"Gone first lady!" Renee started clowning and teasing as always.

"Stop it! Child, I'm not about to be a first nothing…" She laughed.

After their girl talk, Ty'nae got Stormy ready and headed for home. Before she pulled off she checked her cell phone and had a missed call from Seth. She listened to his deep voice on the voice mail. He had called to make sure her and Stormy was home safely. She put on her Bluetooth, dialed his number and as she pulled out of Renee's drive way he answered.

"Did I wake you?" She asked as soon as he said hello with that deep sexy voice that made her blush.

"No ma'am, I was waiting up to hear from you."

"How sweet! Thanks. I just picked up Stormy and we are about twenty minutes from home."

"Okay, so are you holding a cellphone or wearing a Bluetooth?" He was already showing concern towards her.

"Bluetooth, I have precious cargo in the car with me…"

"I'm just making sure. So did you enjoy yourself tonight?" He inquired.

"Yes, it was fun. I hope you enjoyed yourself as well."

"I did. I was hoping that my past wouldn't make you run."

"No, we all have one you know?"

"Is that right?" Seth said sarcastically.

Ty'nae laughed at him, "Yes, that is right mister."

"So, since I'm a keep you company until you get home safely, why don't you tell me about yours? Can you start with telling me if Stormy's father is in the picture?"

Ty'nae hadn't prepared for that topic to come up. She got all jittery at the thought of discussing the matter. Seth had been so free in sharing his own personal truths, she didn't want to shut him out but she truly didn't want to let thoughts of Ryan hold her in bondage. She had come so far.

Ty'nae struggled to find the words to answer Seth. He discerned that she was uncomfortable.

"Hey, listen I am so sorry. That was probably asking for a little too much too soon. I didn't mean to make you uncomfortable."

"It's okay; I want to be able to talk about it. It's just hard."

"I understand. So are you almost home yet?" He tried to change the subject.

"Not really, but once I get to the highway, it's a quick shot."

"The baby is sleep, I assume?"

"Yeah, she wasn't too happy when I picked her up. Renee thinks she has an ear infection. I'm a get her in to the doctor soon." Ty'nae sighed. A mother's work was never ever done.

"Well, if I can do anything to help just let me know." Seth was sincere.

"So, what about your son? Do you go to Kansas City to see him often?" Ty'nae inquired. But by the time the words got out of her mouth, she felt bad to question him about his son when she wasn't willing to talk about Stormy's dad.

"Actually, I see him very often. He stays with me on Spring Break, Thanksgiving and Christmas. I travel to see him on some weekends and now that he is older, his mom sends him here to visit on the Mega Bus sometimes. His mom gave up the special holidays because in the summer her job sends her out of the country and she takes Bo Jangles with her. He is 13 and has been to Europe eleven times to my one!"

"Lol, Bo Jangles huh? Why do you call him that?" Ty'nae found the name endearing.

"He's a Jr., but we never called him Junior… we knew pretty early that he would sing and dance. He is not much of an athlete but he thinks he is

Michael Jackson or somebody. He has been in multiple talent shows. The nick name Bo Jangles just seemed to fit him."

"I like it!" She laughed.

"Now, I remember hearing you sing and play the drums at a service before. So he gets his talent from you, right?" She asked smiling.

"I guess. His mom is a pretty good singer too. Guess he was destined to carry a tune. Now the dancing part he gets from me most definitely. You saw my moves." He laughed at himself remembering his antics on the dance floor.

"Yes, you got moves!" She laughed.

"And Stormy, where did you get her name from?" Seth inquired.

"A childhood friend of mine, but damn if the name doesn't describe my life." The cuss word flew out her mouth before she knew it.

Seth didn't seem to be uptight about it and she was glad. She knew she had a long way to go and grow in her faith. She was nothing like her mother and grandmother in the faith. They never cussed, danced, lied, drank…but to be honest, neither one of them had ever really lived. They were so stuck in a box, always judging others who didn't fit inside of the box with them. Ty'nae loved God and she trusted that many of her still known sins would eventually fall off. She was already proud that she wasn't smoking and even though it wasn't the life she'd chosen, she wasn't shacking up with no man any more either. To be honest, not only was she not having any sex, she wasn't even masturbating.

When Ryan first left she had indulged a few times but soon abandoned that useless habit as well. She smiled as she thought about the changes that God had brought to her life. She wasn't who she wanted to be but she wasn't who she used to be. She had hope of being a woman of God and she longed to be pleasing in God's sight not mans.

"A stormy life, huh?" Seth said longing to know more about how a beautiful woman could describe her life as stormy.

Then, Ty'nae pulled up in her drive way. It was dark and she was glad that the motion sensor light was still working. She grabbed the diaper bag and put her small purse inside of it. She reached behind her and unstrapped Stormy. She didn't want to get out and have her back turned to get her out so while still in the car, she turned her body around enough to reach for Stormy and put her on her chest. She took a thin blanket and put it over Stormy because the night air had turned a little chilly even though it had been blazing hot during the day.

"I'm about to go in the house. I won't talk until I'm in the door because I'm watching my environment. "

"Okay." Seth said and he listened as Ty'nae closed the car door and put her key in the door. He heard the house door shut and the two locks were turned on the door. Then he heard keys placed on a hard surface, presumably a table or counter and he heard her switch on a light and it sounded like she was shuffling something as she walked then he heard Stormy crying at the top of her lungs.

"Shh. Shh. shhhh…it's okay. Come on let momma get these clothes off of you." Ty'nae still hadn't said a word to Seth and he was waiting patiently.

Ty'nae removed a soiled pamper from Stormy and replaced it with a fresh one. She put a little sleeper on her baby and wiped her face and hands with a wet wipe. She checked the diaper bag to see if Renee had put all the bottles back in the compartment. She found one that was ready to use and plopped down on the couch with Stormy and put the bottle to her mouth. She let out a sigh as if she was finally settled in.

"Okay, I'm here…are you still there?" She asked Seth.

"I'm still here beautiful." He had thrown that in before he knew it.

"Thanks, how kind…"

"So what is little momma over there fussing about?"

"She just wanted her bottle. She's fighting sleep for real. You should see her eyes close and when I try to take the bottle she opens them and turns her little lip up like she is going to cry again." She laughed. "This girl is a mess."

"I'm glad you made it in safe. So how long will you be up?" He asked.

"Not long. Soon as she shuts it down I'm ready. You wore me out on the dance floor." She smiled remembering the few times they slow danced.

"Girl, you were making them young girls feel shame the way you was throwing down." He smiled remembering how good her body looked in that white sundress and how smooth her skin was. He thought about her afro and those seductive eyes and kissable lips. He wasn't sure if Ty'nae knew just how fine she was.

"Yeah, but unlike them young girls, I will be paying for those moves. I'm feeling it already." She referred to the tightness in her neck and shoulders that needed a man's hands to work out the kinks.

"Well you go ahead and take care of Stormy and get you some rest. Make sure all the doors are locked and I will check of the two of you tomorrow."

"Okay, thanks again for everything. I really enjoyed the night."

"Goodnight." He said.

"Goodnight." Ty'nae yanked the Bluetooth off of her ear and looked down at Stormy who was holding the bottle in her mouth but not sucking it. She just wanted it there. Ty'nae pushed the coffee table back with her foot and reached for a throw she kept in a chair nearby. She covered her and Stormy both in the throw and turned her body so that Stormy would be facing the inside of the couch and she would be on the end. She watched Stormy fight sleep until finally the bottle fell out of her mouth.

Ty'nae knelled on the side of the couch and placed her hands together. She said a prayer for Stormy, she said a prayer for Renee, and she said a prayer for Seth. She prayed about her new business endeavor. She hadn't planned to but before she knew it, she was praying for Ryan and the tears begin to fall.

"…and God, You know where Ryan is at right now. Please put me and Stormy on his mind. Help me to forgive him so that I won't hinder my blessings. I'm not asking for him to come back to me. I am asking that the heart of this father be turned towards his child. I'm praying that he is alive and that whatever is keeping him from his child will be removed. I'm praying in faith and then God I am praying in hope. I hope that through you I will continue to grow in faith. I hope through you I will not harbor bitterness and hatred towards him. I pray through you that my broken heart and wounded spirit will be healed." Ty'nae felt the spirit of God presence. She put her hand on baby Stormy's head.

"I pray that my child will be provided for and that she will not grow up as a fatherless child. If Ryan won't raise her, I trust you to rise up a man of God that will! Some trust in chariots, some trust in horses but I trust in the name of the Lord my God! I put all my faith and all my hope in you. Wash over my soul God and redeem me through and through. I need you to help me to be able to not hurt so badly. Amen."

Ty'nae was still before the Lord after ending her prayer. She wiped away tears and in his presence she just continued to knell when she heard a voice down in her spirit say, "Thy faith has made thee whole."

Ty'nae remembered reading those words in the bible before although she couldn't recall the story exactly but she knew Jesus had told a woman these same words and he healed her body. She kept hearing the Lord say, "Thy faith has made thee whole." Her spirit was lifted, she felt peace rush over her and the tears were cleansing her of all the pain she'd been trying to pretend was no longer there. God was healing her broken heart. She was able to tell God how bad it hurt and ask him to remove the pain and heaviness. She put Stormy in her baby bed and went and got five sheets of paper from her note book. On every page she wrote the same thing in big, bold letters.... 'Thy faith has made thee whole!'

Ty'nae found some tape and taped a sign on her front door…'Thy faith has made thee whole!" She put one on her back door… 'Thy faith has made thee whole!' Next, she put one on Stormy's bedroom door… 'Thy faith has made thee whole!" She put one on her refrigerator… 'Thy faith has made thee whole!' Then she went to her bathroom, she taped the last sign on one side of her mirror. She stood back and read the words and as she read them she looked at herself in the mirror. Ty'nae was taking back her power, her heart, her emotions, and her mind from the devil. She declared and decreed the word that God had spoken to her, the word she would have to use to fight the devil every day, the word she would recite every time the name Ryan tried to break her down to tears. Her hope in God had healed her… 'Thy faith has made thee whole!"

6 VISION IS CLEAR

Over the next few months, Ty'nae and Seth had started to see each other regularly. Two Friday nights a month became their night out for dancing and enjoying live bands throughout the area. Seth was so thoughtful that he had arranged things with Renee to babysit Stormy on those nights and he paid her out of his own pocket. Renee had no problem watching Stormy. She was assured that God was working things out and sending Ty'nae a godly man that knew her worth.

On one particular night out, Seth just didn't seem himself. He'd always been so talkative and the first to grab Stormy's hand to head towards the dance floor. On this night, he seemed exhausted and as if his mind was far away. Evangeline's on the Central West End was so crowded. The smell of New Orleans cuisine was an aroma that made Ty'nae's appetite grow larger. She was enjoying Crawfish Carolyn. The taste of Louisiana crawfish tails with brandy cream sauce, parmesan and French bread was sending her taste buds straight to heaven. Seth hadn't even touched his Mussels Sauvignon. On stage was Miss Jubilee, a local 60's swing artist. Her performance was excellent and Ty'nae sung along with each song in between taking in her hearty meal.

She didn't want to act ungrateful for their date, but wondered why Seth hadn't cancelled if he didn't want to be there. "You haven't touched your meal much." She said as she tried to make friendly conversation. Seth just cracked a halfhearted smile and stared towards the stage. Miss Jubilee's band played an old time favorite, Pitter Panther Patter and the crowd was rocking back and forth. Ty'nae felt the chords in her soul and wanted to get on the floor and sway her hips. She took another look at Seth and knew that wouldn't be happening. "Seth, what's wrong? I am worried about you. Are you feeling well?" Seth took a deep breath and sipped his *PAINKILLER* drink. The sugar island coconut light rum, dark rum, pineapple juice, orange juice and cream helped to numb the pain he didn't want to feel. As he spoke, his voice cracked sending feelings of compassion straight towards Stormy heart. "It's my son. I have failed as a father." Although the music and energy of the room remained the same, Ty'nae entered the space of Seth's mind. She pulled her chair closer and reached for his hand. Nothing else mattered but him. He was obviously hurting. "Talk to me, Seth. What is wrong? You are definitely not yourself tonight." Being close to him she couldn't help but inhale the citrus, bergamot, rose and musk from his cologne. He smelled good enough to succumb to every sexual urge she felt for him, but they had already agreed to date in God's way which meant no sex. "Would you mind if we cut the night short?" Seth requested. He didn't want to disappoint Ty'nae and even though he wasn't up for talking or dancing he actually liked the light in her eyes that always glistened when she was enjoying good music. Their shared music taste was one of the things he really liked about their new found companionship. Ty'nae didn't mind leaving. They quickly squared their bill and was soon in the car headed to pick up Stormy. They drove in silence. Seth hadn't even turned on the CD player. Ty'nae honestly didn't know what to say and didn't want to force him to talk. Before long, Seth veered in a different direction and Ty'nae knew they were not off to Renee's place just yet. She looked out of her window at large brick homes with big porches and well-manicured lawns. Some of the properties were so immaculate that Ty'nae couldn't even imagine how much it would cost to live in such a home. After several winding roads and a long path leading to a gate, Seth parked. He got out of the car and went around to Ty'nae's side to help her out. Through the gate, she could see a small pond and lots of small bushes. "I worked in this area a few years ago. See that house over there…I painted it." He said as he pointed beyond the *No Trespassing* sign. The house was so big and beautiful and had a widow's door on the top balcony. Ty'nae loved the architecture and wished she could get a better look, but from where she was standing in the near dark she couldn't take in much. If not for all the yard lights she'd barely see the little bench closer to the pond. They walked towards the bench to sit and Ty'nae hoped that no one would call the police on them. After all, they were obviously out of their neighborhood.

"Bo Jangles…" Seth's voice cracked again, "His mom says he is very sick." Ty'nae put her hand on Seth's leg and patting him, "I wouldn't consider you as a failure because of a sick kid." She wasn't being dismissive, but knew it had to be way more to justify the melancholy behavior Seth was displaying. "He is 13 years old and his mother just found out that he has diabetes. I feel like I have failed him because I should be there. I should be raising my son every day and not just seeing him on occasional weekends and school breaks. Soon as she told me, I started feeling like I have missed out on so much of his life." Ty'nae felt his sadness and she leaned against him putting her head on his shoulder. Softly she responded, "Seth, we can't control what life throws at us. It's not your fault that you are co-parenting from out of town. It's life."

"It is my fault, Ty'nae. First of all, I should have done better by his mother. I told you about my criminal past, but I also just didn't respect women much. Sleeping with this one and that one without trying to be seriously committed and all. Then, my son came. I thought about marrying his mom so that we could be a family, but my heart just wouldn't let me. I have always been in my son's life. I feel like with him being there and me here, it makes it harder to know about his day to day encounters. I see him as much as I can and his mom has never played games or tried to keep me from him. She takes him out the country a lot because of her job. I am not sure if I want him going as much now that we know he has diabetes. I really just feel burdened Ty'nae. I think I want to take on my son full time."

Ty'nae listened attentively. She could tell that Seth was really pondering the future and wanted what was best for his son. He had a clear vision for the future he desired for him and his son. He was trying to figure it all out in terms of how to execute the vision. That was admirable and touched Ty'nae's heart deeply. Hesitantly, Seth spoke, "It's just that...well, and I have to figure it all out. I am still not where I want to be financially. His mom actually makes way more money than I do and I pay her child support. I don't want to bring him here and not be able to provide the life he is used to. I am feeling defeated because nothing matters to me more than Bo Jangles." Ty'nae hugged Seth tight and kissed his cheek. He turned his face so that his lips could meet hers and they savored their first kiss. Ty'nae used her mouth to bring calmness to Seth's weary soul. She put both of her hands on his face as she brought him closer and deeper. Her lips were like honey to a bee. His skin soft. She believed in him. She believed that he would do whatever he needed to in order to get his son and make things comfortable. She felt deeply attracted to his desire to be a father and care for his son. She felt attracted to his concern for his son. She felt like she wanted to be the one to encourage him and support him in his endeavor. Seth hadn't felt a woman's touch and caress in a few years. He hadn't even allowed himself to search out a woman because he was so focused on his relationship with God, rebuilding his life and accepting his call to the ministry. Ty'nae's lips on his caused his manhood to harden. He was determined to date God's way. He kept thinking that if kissing her felt so good that his penis throbbed there was no doubt that they had sexual chemistry. He didn't want to pull away but at one point felt he would bust if he didn't. He pulled away, but didn't want to let go of her. They sat with their hands intertwined in silence. Ty'nae was breathing heavy. She was wet between her legs and battling the strong desire to unclothed right there in their little simulated Garden of Eden. "What are you thinking?" asked Seth. "I'm not." she was being honest. "Just floating mister, you got me just floating." Seth got up quick before he acted out of his flesh and walked them back to the car. No sooner as he got her in the car and walked to his side to get in, Ty'nae was ready to fuck. She had already unbuttoned her blouse and reached for his hand to touch her hard nipple. Seth fought hard. He was weak, but determined. "Ty'nae! Button your blouse!" He pulled his hand away. She felt embarrassed and ashamed until she heard him laugh. "What am I going to do with a woman like you?" He laughed again as he beat his head against the headrest. "Girl, you are fine as hell and I want you so bad, but you know we got to do this right. Lord, help us do this thing right." He started the car and Ty'nae started laughing as she looked at him out the corner of her eye and bite her lip. "Yeah, you better pray Seth. Pray hard. You almost got it!" She rolled her eyes playfully. She was glad he had control or she would have been repenting of fornication for sure. Seth was pressing all of her buttons without trying. He was fine, honest and trying to do the right things. All of those attributes combined were a turn on. She hoped He could stay strong because she doubted her ability to reframe.

7 NO MORE TEARS

Ties were selling! The word was out! Ty'nae was pulling in way more money than she had ever imagined, but with a baby, a full time job and a dating life there was just no way she could spend as much time making ties by hand and filling orders. She revisited her church notes that had been the foundation of her tie business.

1. We all have been given gifts and talents to share with the world.
2. Those gifts are to aid the body of Christ, but also to assist us in becoming financially empowered.
3. Identify things you enjoy and evaluate if you can use it as a ministry or a business.
4. Ask Holy Spirit to allow you to take that thing which you have identified before people who can make it bigger and better than you ever imagined.

She had made enough money to not only pay Renee back the seed money she had given her, but to also start paying full price for Stormy's daycare cost. Renee didn't want full price but Ty'nae insisted. She never wanted Renee to feel as if she was taking her for granted. Also,

Renee had gone above the call of duty by also watching Stormy so that Seth could take her out on dates.

Seth was doing what he needed to do to get his ducks in a row so that his son could come live with him permanently. Bo Jangles mother was open to the idea. She felt like her son was at a good age to be placed entirely in his father's care and this would allow her to soar in her career even more.

Things had progressed to Seth visiting Ty'nae's place regularly. Initially, he felt bad that she lived in a home so much nicer than his own. Yet, he was doing his best. He was saving money, paying off debts, putting money aside for bible school and doing all he could to prepare for his son. He was also, unbeknown to Ty'nae saving for a ring. They hadn't been dating long, but it didn't take long to hear God's voice during his times of prayer. He not only wanted to raise his own son fulltime, he longed to be Ty'nae's husband and Stormy's dad. He was filled with so much anger every time he thought of how Ryan could have abandoned Stormy. There was just no reason to abandon your own flesh and blood in his opinion. He could understand breaking up with a woman; after all, he was notorious for loving and leaving before finding Christ, but never a child. Every child needed a father and since Ryan had neglected to be one, Seth was more than willing to step into those shoes. Every time he looked into baby Stormy eyes he fell deeper in love with the thought of raising her as his own. Every time he spent time with Ty'nae her smile, eyes and warm caress made him feel like a real man. He wanted to be her provider, protector and the priest God ordained for her life.

Ty'nae struggled to not move too fast with Seth. She kept telling herself to focus on being a mom and her new business. She sat at her little desk reviewing her scriptures and sermon notes. Her evaluation caused her to check off most of the steps on the list. The only thing left was trying to find someone to help her take her business further than she could ever imagine. It was a long shot. The ties were selling fast but Ty'nae worried that it would be a fast fleeting trend. She didn't know if she should attempt to do more or not. She bowed her head to pray for her business, her baby and her *boo thing* as Renee always called Seth. She wanted God's guidance. She also prayed for Ryan. He still hadn't called, sent a letter or anything. Ty'nae was moving on with her life and it seemed as if God was blessing her in spite of Ryan's absence. She just worried about Stormy not growing up with her dad.

Renee had been in her prayer closet seeking God's face. Her day care was doing well and she was extremely happy to be able to lend a helping hand to Ty'nae. It seemed as if every time she prayed over Ty'nae she heard the Lord speaking so clearly concerning a quick work in her life. Renee knew all too well that God had a way of redeeming time in a way man couldn't always understand. She also knew that the fires of ministry were ignited in Seth's heart. She would cry out to God to give them both direction. She was very concerned if Ty'nae would receive her destiny with joy. God was showing Renee that soon Ty'nae would have to leave her job. She would not experience lack. God was going to use her new business to provide miraculously. God needed Ty'nae's time so that His perfect work in Seth's life could be fulfilled. So many men needed Seth to take his position in ministry. Young boys going astray would benefit greatly from Seth's testimony and his mentorship skills. To be his wife, Ty'nae would need to be ministry minded. Renee knew that Ty'nae was still a babe in Christ in many ways. Although she had committed her life back to God, she wasn't as sold out as she needed to be for the work God was about to send her forth to do; the work of ministry beside her husband. Every time, God showed Renee that Seth was Ty'nae's husband she got excited. She knew that God was dealing with Seth's heart, but it was Ty'nae that exhausted her in prayer and travailing. God had to destroy some yokes and break some chains in order for Ty'nae to see clearly.

After her time of prayer, Ty'nae made phone calls, made a list of things to do and set a few business goals to accomplish over the course of a month. Things were so hectic; she knew she had to follow a schedule to stay on task. She checked on her beautiful baby, sat out her work clothes and finally crawled into bed. Thoughts of Seth mesmerized her mind, making it hard to go to sleep. She kept thinking about how fun he was to be around, how intense his passion for the Lord was and how steadfast he was in making changes in order to get his son. He was a man on a mission to get his house in order and Ty'nae loved that about him. She had to be honest with herself and conclude that although she hadn't known him very long, she loved him. She loved him as a person, friend and knew she desired him as a lover. Thoughts of abandonment caused feelings of low self-esteem to creep in, but she fought those feelings by reminding herself of all the times that Seth had called her smart, beautiful, and the many times he fought back taking her to bed in order to honor God. She felt respected by him. She felt like she could trust him with her heart and that he wouldn't intentionally hurt her. Yet, when she closed her eyes she saw Ryan…his absence was a torment.

8 LOVE ME NOW

More months passed and amazing things were happening. Ty'nae found a reputable company that would produce her ties in bulk and distribute them to two stores, Aldo's and K & G. Ty'nae contracted with a local sports store to make team ties for sport's banquets. She was starting to build a name in her local area. Renee had helped her get into vending events amongst other groups of women entrepreneurs and Ty'nae was living her life like it was golden. Now with a regular job and a business that was bringing in a decent cash flow, Ty'nae was caught up on her bills. Stormy was getting big and it seemed like she was constantly buying clothes to fit her. Seth was still being all the man she could have ever prayed for plus more. His son Seth Jr. was in town and she normally called him that instead of his nick name. She didn't want to come off as if she was already that close to him for fear of pushing him away. She didn't want him to feel as if she was replacing his mom in any way. His stay still wasn't permanent, but his dad was arranging more weekend visits. Ty'nae and baby Stormy would hit the high way with him to pick up and drop off his son in Columbia, MO. At first, Ty'nae was afraid to meet Seth Jr.'s mom, but to her surprise she was very nice. She welcomed Ty'nae with a hug instead of a hand shake and seemed fine with the fact that her son's father had a girlfriend. *Girlfriend,* Ty'nae could pinch herself at the thought that she was Seth's girlfriend. The whole church knew by now that they were an item. Seth had been taking minister's training with his pastor and a few other brothers. He'd enrolled in an on-line bible school and was talking to Ty'nae about his plans for the future. She noticed that whenever he spoke future tense, he included her. "I was thinking we'd stay in your area because the schools are so much better for Stormy and Bo Jangles." "I have been looking at mini vans and thinking of getting us one." She got the picture he was painting and really liked seeing herself in the portrait.

She really liked the times when him and his son would be at her house and his son would play with Stormy. Her baby girl loved the attention and would laugh a lot when Seth Jr. was around. They were bonding in their own way. Although, Seth Jr. had diabetes he seemed just as active as other kids his age. He would show them his tap dancing steps he'd practiced for an upcoming talent show. He was so talented. He had gentlemen ways and was such a respectful young man. Traveling the world with his mom made him so cultured and Ty'nae loved that he would speak both English and Spanish when interacting with Stormy. There was such calmness when they all were together and Ty'nae saw something in her man's eyes…Peace. He was happy. He was such a giving man and for that Ty'nae was grateful.

One day, all of them were enjoying their peaceful time together when the doorbell rang. Ty'nae never ever had company. She didn't really deal with people like that apart from Renee, who would never show up unannounced unless it was an emergency. Seth heard the doorbell and noticed Ty'nae didn't move quickly. She felt uneasy. Seth, went to the door and inquired of who was on the other side. No one spoke and without a peek hole Seth couldn't tell who rang the bell. Seth motioned for Bo Jangles to take Stormy to her room and Ty'nae moved close to Seth. Seth opened the door but no one was there. He looked all around and there was no one. He closed the door and looked at the paralyzing look in Ty'nae's eyes. "I bet it was him." She said with a perplexed look on her face. Seth didn't say a word. He just pulled her close and held her tight. His lips met hers and he could feel her trembling as if she was afraid. "Ty'nae, it doesn't matter if he comes back or not. We will get through it together." She held on to his words but that didn't stop the anxiety she felt. He kissed her again as if to remind her that he meant every word he'd said about getting through it all together. Then again to persist that she listened. Then again he pressed his lips against hers and gave in to the comfort of his mouth, his tongue, his tight embrace. When their lips parted Bo Jangles was watching with Stormy in his arms. He walked close to them and said, "Group hug!" and they laughed. The tension was gone from the room and they went on with their evening.

Seeing Seth and his son out the door at the end of the night was so hard for her. Partly because she didn't want them to leave and partly because she was afraid that a knock would come to the door and Seth wouldn't be there to answer. It had been almost 7 months since she'd last seen Ryan face to face. She was so mad at him. Not because of what he did to her, but the disregard he showed towards his daughter. So many nights, Ty'nae had thought of trying to reach out to his mother but they didn't have any kind of relationship. Involving his mother as if he was a little boy would only make things worse. Ryan was a grown man that had walked out on his responsibility. Although he never took money out of their shared account, he hadn't added any either so he wasn't even providing for his child. One part of Ty'nae wished he would come knocking so she could cuss him out comfortably without her bible quoting boyfriend present. The other side of her kept thinking that she was clueless of Ryan's mental state and wasn't sure if her and Stormy would be safe if he showed up. She couldn't wait to call Renee.

Renee sounded so exhausted on the other end that Ty'nae felt guilty for waking her up. "I am not sleep just tired." Renee insisted when Ty'nae apologized and offered to call another time. "No, really, I'm good. What's up?" Renee asked. "Girl, I think Stormy's dad came by today." Renee sat straight up in the bed. The Lord had showed her earlier that Stormy's dad would make an appearance. She knew that when you were on the verge of a breakthrough satan got busy. She had spent time in prayer rebuking the darts of the wicked one that would come against Ty'nae and Seth. Hearing Ty'nae tell the story was only confirmation for what Renee had seen in the spirit. She had seen some deeper things she wanted to share with Ty'nae but the Lord hadn't released her to tell her, just to pray for her. Renee had a conformation from God that Ryan's abandonment was more of a blessing than Ty'nae realized. He was mentally and emotionally unstable and that would have only made things worse. Sometimes when people are wrestling demons, they purposely separate themselves from those they don't want to hurt. Ryan may have seemed cruel to abruptly abandon Stormy, but he had spent much time mentally reflecting on how his secret habits would impact her life.

God was intentional in everything that was unfolding in Ty'nae's life. Sometimes, we fail to see that the writing on the wall is so plain and clear. God was keeping Ty'nae and Stormy in his safety.

Two more weeks passed and there had been no more knocks on the door. Ty'nae had let her guards down and wasn't' feeling as much anxiety. Seth was proving to be a true man of God with a heart of love and understanding and she was melting in the glow of his love and consistency. Seth's son's mom had agreed to allow their child to move in full time with his dad in a few more months and pastor had scheduled an ordination day to formally give Seth a minister's license. Ty'nae still couldn't believe that a flat tire after church had ushered her into the arms of a man who loved God, studied God's word and desired to serve Him with all of his heart. She was also very grateful that although Seth was undeniably a man of God, he also had other interest and lived a normal, balanced life. Ty'nae could be herself. He wasn't trying to force her into being the first lady type. He loved her and as long as she supported the call on his life and loved him back, Seth was a happy man.

Running late to work due to running her mouth at Renee's, Ty'nae knew her boss would not be happy. Things at work had taken on a change. People at the office seemed to withdraw from her more and her boss was always pressing her to produce more and more work with the same pay. She couldn't put her finger on what was really going on but it seemed like her boss and a few co-workers had a little attitude towards her. She had talked to Renee about it. Renee told her to trust in the Lord and lean not on her on understanding. Ty'nae had just rolled her eyes, because she just couldn't live like Renee. Renee was ever the encourager full of God's word, but sometimes, Ty'nae just wanted her to get on her level and agree with her desire to just cuss a few people at work out.

Ty'nae clocked in a few minutes late and once she got to her desk, before she could even put her purse down, her boss came into her office. "I need to speak with you once you are settled in!" she breezed in and out the door with a nasty attitude. Mrs. Rizzle was on one, but Ty'nae just gave her a side eye. Ty'nae hadn't even had the chance to respond and was somewhat offended that her boss hadn't even said good morning. She put her things away and headed towards her bosses office. She could see a few nosey eyes watching her and knew that nothing good was about to happen. "Take a seat, Ty'nae" her boss said. Ty'nae noticed the unfriendly look on her face and the sternness in her voice and knew she was upset about way more than a tardy punch on the clock. "Ty'nae, this isn't personal. Unfortunately, it has come to my attention that you have been using the company's computer for your personal use. This is a direct failure to comply with company rules." Ty'nae didn't know what to say. She had indeed looked up a thing or two on the company computer but had not gone as far to be considered abusing her company's policy in her opinion. "Here is a copy of what concerns us." Her boss showed her a printout indicating that Ty'nae had searched for information on fabric and supplies to make her ties. There was also evidence that she had ordered and had things shipped to her home address. Ty'nae hadn't thought she was doing much wrong. "I did do both of these things. However, this is not something I do regularly. I apologize and will not do it anymore." Mrs. Rizzle took a deep breath, "Listen, I know that you didn't mean anything by this and hate I have to be the one to approach you. However, you need to be mindful that when these things occur, I have a boss too that is on my back. I don't like to be questioned about things going on in my department. I will say from my stand point this is petty, but it lets me know that someone isn't happy about the fact that there are a lot of people walking around this company sporting your ties. Ty'nae, I must ask that you not sale anymore of your ties here at the office. I am sorry, but you must keep the two separate. Also, I need you to get to work on time. I notice you've been slacking. At first, I wasn't going to say anything because I know how it is trying to get a baby to the sitter before work. However, when people start to take notice then I have to say something." Ty'nae understood. She couldn't be mad because she was guilty. She also knew that her boss had initially been very open to her selling her ties at the office, so the heat was coming from somewhere else in the department. She had sold plenty of ties at work and had set a great trend that the men and women loved. Someone was jealous and Ty'nae had to shake the devil off. She knew that it was a hater's job to hate and she was going to be just fine because she was already set up to sell on line. Those who wanted to support her still would do so, and nothing could stop what God had in store for her.

Back at her desk, Ty'nae busied herself and even turned on some soft music to help set her pace. She loved Pandora and had decided to use the Erykah Badu station. The neo soul turned down low was just enough to focus her on things that she had to complete. Lost in her work she hadn't even noticed how fast time was passing until someone came into her office. Bob was a man of few words. He was kind but quiet. "Hey, there are subway sandwiches in the breakroom. You better come out of hiding before their all gone." Ty'nae hadn't been informed that the office was providing lunch but was happy to have a free meal. She thanked Bob for being considerate enough to inform her and made her way to the break room. She smiled as she entered the room to see at least two people with her ties on. She went to the sink to wash her hands, grabbed a plate and napkin and fell in line behind a few others. "How's your baby girl?" Cindy, one of the front desk receptionists asked. "Big as ever! She will be one soon."

"Wow, time passed fast."

Ty'nae smiled, "You got that right! I would love it to slow down. I am enjoying her at this age." Both women made it to the spread of food and filled their plates. The woman moved to grab a seat amongst co-workers, but Ty'nae ever the loner decided to take her plate back to her office so she could call Seth.

She closed the door slightly behind her, sat her desk and took a huge bite out of her sandwich. She pulled open the chips and dialed up Seth. All he heard was potato chips crunching in his ear.

"I hope it's good!" He said and Ty'nae snickered.

"I was trying to finish chewing to say hi…" she laughed… "How's it going handsome?"

"Pretty well, very pretty lady" Ty'nae blushed.

Their short conversation left them both blushing and Ty'nae couldn't wait to get off of work and see Seth's face. During their short talk they'd agreed to do dinner at his place. For the first time, Seth had asked if he could pick up Stormy from Renee's house. Ty'nae was taken back by the request and didn't know how to reply. However, she knew that Seth loved her and they had been dating long enough for her to trust him. She agreed and sent a text to Renee to inform her that Seth would pick up Stormy. Ty'nae would grab dinner and they'd meet up at Seth's. She was excited. She was also happy to know that she could finish up her work without having to rush. Since Seth was picking up Stormy, she had an additional hour to get things done. Having help felt so good. Being in love was a wonderful thing and having a good man made it so much easier to handle her business.

Later that evening, Ty'nae rested in Seth's arms after devouring chicken marsala with white pasta that she'd picked up from the Pasta House. Baby Stormy crawled around the floor playing with a toy. Things felt peaceful and right. Seth's strong arms caressed her in such a protective and loving manner that Ty'nae wanted to remain engulfed in the feelings forever.

"Thank you." Seth said out of the blue.

"You are welcomed. I hope you enjoyed the meal."

"I did. But I am more thankful for you trusting me to pick up Stormy." Seth told her that Renee had already had all of Stormy's stuff ready at the door and that she was smiling ear to ear when he arrived at the door. Ty'nae laughed as Seth told her about how Mookie didn't want Stormy to go with him. She had started crying and even tried to pull Stormy out of his arms. She kept saying, "You not her mommy! You not her mommy!" Both of them laughed and Ty'nae said, "Mookie was on her stranger danger post!" Although she had seen Seth many times, she'd never known him to pick up Stormy alone. Mookie was looking out for baby Stormy. Ty'nae had already heard a part of the story from Renee who had video chatted with her soon as Seth had left with Stormy.

"Giiiiiirl, that man loves you! He had his chest out honey. Picking up his daughter! That's your boo, honey!" Ty'nae knew Renee was a mess. She had already started calling Seth Stormy's daddy."

Renee had put Mookie on to the video chat so that Ty'nae could tell Mookie that Stormy was safe and that she had told Seth to pick her up. Mookie seemed to be better after seeing Ty'nae on the video chat saying that it was okay.

In Seth's arms Ty'nae was comfortable. Stormy became frustrated with her toy and soon crawled near them begging to be picked up by whining and lifting her arms. Seth reached down to scoop Stormy up with one hand and she started to giggle. He had both of his ladies in his arms and the world felt just right.

9 SUNSHINE

Months passed and before long it was the day of Stormy's birthday. Renee was so extra with all the stuff she had ordered for the backyard party she was planning. She had invited all the little kids from the day care and a few from the church nursery. Ty'nae had told her she was going too far, but Renee was claiming Stormy as her godchild. With her hands on her hips she stood at the cake counter at Sam's waiting patiently for the finishing touches to be put on the cake she had made with a baby picture of Stormy on it. "Girl, look you only live once. I think we should get a snow cone machine too." Ty'nae gave Renee the look. "I think enough is enough. She is still too young to understand what is really going on. This is your party not hers." Ty'nae laughed

"O' then if that's the case honey we are definitely getting a snow cone machine!" Ty'nae knew not to protest. Renee was spending her own money.

Seth called right as they were leaving Sam's to inform them that all the decorations were up and that Bo Jangles wanted to know which side of the yard Ms. Renee wanted the small pool to be on. The back yard looked cluttered with stuff. Everyone agreed that Renee was doing too much but no one could stop her. She loved to entertain. She loved to see children happy. She wanted Stormy to have a great party.

Once they arrived at Renee's house, Seth and Bo Jangles came out to help get bags. Bo Jangles held Stormy's hand until it was secured in Ty'nae's. Stormy didn't want to let his hands go. They had become so attached. He kissed her and said, "Go to momma, Stormy. I have to get these bags." It took a few times before she complied and Ty'nae was just about to tap her legs if she didn't. Seth and his son had Stormy so spoiled it was pitiful. Matter of fact, along with Renee, Stormy had an abundance of love and attention. Ty'nae was happy with her circle of love.

Kids and parents arrived, the clown was entertaining and after a few hours the kids were in the pool with parents assisting. The day was warm and the sun was bright and Stormy kept eyeing how Seth and his son interacted with her daughter. Ty'nae kept thinking about how blessed she was to have the love of a man who went the extra mile for her doing his best to show her affection. Seth didn't have much in terms of material but he had reached many goals including finally having his son living with him. Mookie's dad approached Seth and Ty'nae at the party. "Hey, I have been wanted to talk to you." He extended his handshake to both of them, but then focused his gaze on Ty'nae. "Listen, I met this guy from New York that works in the fashion district. He has been designing suits for men for many years. The day I met him, I was wearing one of your ties that Renee gave me as a gift. We struck up a good conversation and he wants to talk to you. This guy is the truth Ty'nae. I think he can help take your business further than you ever imagined!" He handed her a business card and encouraged her to not sleep on making the call. Ty'nae thanked him and Seth did as well. Ty'nae quickly referred back to her ministry notes #4 came to mind as clear as day, "Ask Holy Spirit to allow you to take that thing which you have identified before people who can make it bigger and better than you ever imagined."

Ty'nae knew that God was moving. Seth felt the same. He hugged her tight, "I am proud of what God is doing in your life beautiful." He kissed her lips and Ty'nae didn't shy away. She loved public displays of affection. She was proud of her man of God and felt so humbled that he loved and respected her the way he did. So often, she wanted to get undressed and put her flesh on his, but he honored her constantly. She was happy he was a man of control because she wasn't as strong. She hadn't told him, but there had been a few times after he'd left she had to masturbate. She couldn't contain the fire he kindled between her legs. He didn't have to try, it was his presence alone and how transparent they could be in conversation. Even with Ryan, she hadn't disclosed as much about her inner self as she had with Seth. He knew her. He knew that she loved God, but battled with doubts and fears. He also knew she was afraid to be abandoned. He wasn't planning on ever doing that. He wanted to be the stability that she and Stormy could grow to trust always. The son of God was moving in their life and the sunshine on Ty'nae's face made her glow. They were in love.

Later, that night Ty'nae was settled in at home in the comfort of her bed. She was so exhausted when she had gotten home that she had left all of Stormy's birthday presents in the car. Although Seth had wanted to unload them, she insisted that they would be just fine remaining in the truck for the night. Bo Jangles helped to get Stormy in bed. He read her a story, sung a song and eventually fell off to sleep in the chair next to her bed. Ty'nae didn't bother to wake him. She put a blanket over him and suggested that Seth and he just stay the night. Seth insisted that he'd take the couch and Ty'nae's back was so sore she knew she had to get in her bed. She pulled her covers up tight and closed her eyes. She prayed to God thanking him for blessing Stormy to see her first birthday. She thanked him for Seth and Bo Jangles. Her eyes filled with tears when she prayed for Renee. She had a family now although, it wasn't official. She prayed and asked God if it ever would be official. She knew that Seth had been making changes intentionally, but he hadn't asked her to marry him. She wondered if she was getting too comfortable being his girlfriend. After all, the man was on her couch snoring so loud she wanted to put a pillow over his head. She swore he'd wake up the children.

Ty'nae eased into sleep and out of the blue was awaken by the sound of arguing. She could hear voices and was in a panic.

"Dude, I will kill your mother fucking ass!"

"You don't run a damn thing up in here anymore! Get your bitch ass out of here!"

Stormy was crying and Bo Jangles was holding her tight in his arm as they stood in the hallway watching Seth and Ryan go at it.

Ty'nae could hardly believe her eyes. She glanced at the clock on the wall in the kitchen nearby. It was 3:17 a.m. She had been sleeping so hard she hadn't heard a knock at the door or anything. All she heard was Seth cussing and Ryan trying to explain.

"Look, I didn't know you live here. I just wanted to see my daughter. It's her birthday, man."

"First of all, it's none of your business if I live here or not! Why the fuck you coming here at this time of morning? And how the hell is it you think it's ok to show up for her birthday but you have been a mother fucking disappearing act from her life! Get your ass out of here!"

Ty'nae reached for Seth's hand just as he was about to ball up his fist to blacken Ryan's eye. "Calm down, baby, please calm down." Seth charged at Ryan pushing him against the wall and started laying hands like a boxer. Ryan was swinging back but it was no match for Seth's fury. "Dad, stop it! You are upsetting Stormy!" Bo Jangles screamed at the top of his lungs and Stormy was crying and hiding her face in Bo Jangles leg. Seth looked up for a moment to see a scared little girl and his son protecting her and he let Ryan go. "Take her to the room!" He demanded of Seth Jr.

Ryan stayed down. He was rubbing his jaw that felt out of place and he was pleading to Ty'nae. "Look, I am wrong. I know I am wrong. I tried to come by one other time, but a man answered the door. I figured if I came at this hour you wouldn't have company. That's not how you normally do things. I didn't know someone lived here with you."

"He doesn't live here, but that's none of your business! Why are you here?" She reached for Seth's hands and they pulled close as Ryan struggled to stand up. "Not a day goes by that I don't think of Stormy. I wanted to see her. It's her birthday."

"What the fu…" Ty'nae squeezed Seth's hand to silence him before he spewed out more cuss words.

"Look, Ryan, we have moved on. You abandoned us. We haven't heard from you. Your daughter is one years old now. Where have you been the last nine months?"

"Ty'nae, I am sorry and it's so many things I need to tell you. I just want to see my daughter. Please! Please!" He looked at her with pleading eyes and Ty'nae begin to cry.

"NO!" Seth's voice was firm.

"She is my daughter, you have nothing…" Before Ryan could finish his sentence Seth had his hands on his neck.

"Listen, this is how this is going to go down. You are leaving here right this moment. If you want to see my daughter then get a lawyer! If I see you here ever again, I'm going to jail. Whatever is decided in court we will comply with, but don't bring your ass back here!" With his hand still around Ryan's neck, Seth led him to the door. He slammed it so hard once Ryan was out the door that the mirror on the wall fell.

Ty'nae sat on the couch sobbing in disbelief. Seth looked at her, but made his way to the backroom to comfort the children. He was gone a long time and Ty'nae didn't bother to go back to the room to involve herself. When he did come back he had his shirt off. His muscles were glistening and his face still tight with anger. He undid his belt and removed his pants. He reached for Ty'nae who didn't know just how to take seeing him standing there in his boxers reaching for her hand. He pulled her from the couch and held her close.

"Ty'nae, he can't come back. He can't come back!" Seth held Ty'nae for dear life and she felt the wetness of tears from his eyes. The release of pinned up anger, frustrations and now fear came flowing down in tears.

"Tell me you are over him! Tell me that you love me like I love you! He can't come back!"

Ty'nae tried to comfort Seth. Her hands trembled over his muscles as she ran them across his chest. She kissed his tears. She kissed his lips. She accepted his lead to the bedroom. He put her down gently removing her clothes and kissing her softly. He had withheld his passion and did things God's way, but the emotions he felt seeing that man up in her house acting as if he had the right to see her and Stormy made him angry. He realized there was no more time to wait. He had to secure his place in her heart and as her husband. He had to let her know that he wanted to be her everything; he wanted her to know that he was the only father Stormy would ever need. Seth made love to Ty'nae causing her hips to sway in ways she hadn't moved in a long time. They were engulfed in a sexual dance gyrating and thrusting movements brought them both to climax quickly especially since neither of them had had sex in a very long time. Apart of Seth felt guilty for fornicating but another side of him felt vulnerable and thoughts of Ty'nae allowing Ryan back in was playing with his mind. She was his woman. He felt his family being threatened. He knew he had to make it legal. He knew he couldn't let Ryan steal his sunshine! He knew repentance was needed but since he was already wrong up in Ty'nae's bed he decided to not just make love to her, but to fuck her like he had been wanting to ever since that night she had unbutton her shirt and put his hand on her nipples. He felt no guilt about the kids being in the other room. Those were his damn kids, his damn house and his damn woman who he was about to make his wife.

LIKE ME NOW

They say the morning after can be the most uncomfortable for a couple who has crossed the lines prematurely. But, not for Ty'nae and Seth. She woke up before everyone and had breakfast on the table. She was smiling ear to ear and feeling like a million dollars. Having everyone at the kitchen table felt natural. There was love and peace amongst them. She wasn't about to torment herself over the fact that she had sex. God knew it had been hard to withstand and whatever that was that made Seth need to release inside of her she was grateful because the man had skills. She was so turned on by seeing him beat up Ryan and put him out the house she had felt herself moist between the legs as she sat on the couch crying while Seth talked to the kids. She knew that Seth felt guilty, but she knew he'd lead them into prayer for repentance. The bigger issue was now trying to go back to no sex now that she had touched, tasted and felt Seth's manliness inside of her. During breakfast, Seth bowed on one knee in front of Stormy and Bo Jangles and asked Ty'nae to be his wife. He didn't have a ring and she didn't care. She screamed, "Yes!" from the top of her lungs and Stormy and Bo Jangles seemed to be just as happy.

Handling Business

Over the next month, Ty'nae and Seth had made an appointment with the pastor for counseling. He bought Ty'nae a beautiful ring with money he had saved. Renee had helped refer him to a good jeweler that would give him the most for his money. To save money they had decided upon a home wedding and what better place to have it than Renee's house. After all, she was the queen of event planning. Ty'nae had invited her family from Memphis and even included Bo Jangles mother on the guest list. It was to be a simple ceremony with just those close to their heart. Right before the wedding, Ty'nae was asked to fly out to New York to meet with the fashion designer she had been referred to by Mookie's father. She came back totally transformed by the offer he had made to get her ties in stores in New York and to include them in an upcoming fashion show with the top names in men's fashion. The deal was so lucrative that Ty'nae could quit her day job. Seth had brought up in counseling how that God had given him an international mandate which required travel and he wanted Ty'nae by his side. He was honest with the pastor about their act of fornication and had explained the situation. The pastor referred them to a family counselor and advocate that worked with many blended families in the church. Ty'nae and Seth had both sincerely repented and were trying their best to stay away from sex until their wedding. Seth didn't want to waste any time and felt it was way more important to focus on the marriage and not the wedding. Yet, Renee was already walking around with her hands on her hips given out orders on how things would be. Ty'nae told her the colors she wanted and other important things that mattered to her and then basically allowed Renee to work her magic. She trusted her friend. Renee had grown to know her taste. What Ty'nae really wanted for her wedding was a sew-in hair style and she got it! A day at the spa and a new hair -do that matched the new glow on her face was all she needed. She chose a simple dress and made sure the kids had nice attire as well. When the day came she was ready. She had a new son, a new husband, a new company to run and a new ministry to fulfill with the love of her life.

By the time that Ryan had actually gotten a lawyer and revealed that he had abandoned his daughter because of his undercover drug use, both Ty'nae and Seth felt forgiven towards him. He revealed that he had spent time in a rehab and that his friend Sam had helped him get his life clean. Neither Ty'nae nor Seth were ready to let him just come right on in to Stormy's life, but tried to be understanding. Although Ryan had hurt Ty'nae deeply and not been in Stormy's life, he had left for a good reason. He knew he needed to deal with issues that would have brought harm had he stayed. Ryan revealed that his friend Sam had wanted to come by and tell Ty'nae the truth but he had begged him not to because he felt so ashamed. For years he had hid his addiction and the stress of a new baby had sent him down a dark road. He confided in Sam and had checked himself into a facility. Once clean, he still felt too ashamed to return but as Stormy's birthday approached he had gotten up the nerves to try to start over. For the first time, all of Ryan's mood swings and crazy behaviors made sense to Ty'nae. She now understood that he had been battling a drug demon the whole time they were involved.

Ty'nae was strong in her faith. God had done amazing things and was still very much at work in her life. He was making all things new and beautiful and she couldn't help but ask the devil, "How you like me now!" She remembered the way it all begin when Ryan left her and she was drinking her depression away, drowning sorrows in a bottle of whatever could make the pain go away. She remembered that day she felt so much anxiety about not having a babysitter and feared losing her job. She recalled the day Renee had testified to her and volunteered to be Stormy's babysitter. She smiled as she thought about the sermon that day which was the very foundation her business, 'All Tied Up' was built on. She felt waves of passion at memories that flooded her heart about a flat tire and fine dark skinned man coming to her rescue to change her tire. Life was grand. God had handled all of her problems and now as the wife of Minister Seth Jackson, she was ready to handle God's business.

ABOUT THE AUTHOR

DeVonshae Ali resides in St. Louis, MO. She is the mother of Elijah, Isaiah and Joshua. She is very active in her community. Her passion is to help those living with lupus as a spokesperson for the Lupus Foundation of America Heartland Chapter. She has served the organization as an ambassador, featured Face of Lupus, 2014 Campaign Ad Appeal and speaker for Walk to End Lupus Now. DeVonshae has served as a torch lighter for the United Way of Greater St. Louis. DeVonshae is a poet, actress, model and radio show producer. She had been in several independent films, web series and sitcoms.

Ms. Ali knows the personal struggles of single motherhood as she is currently a divorced mom of three living with lupus. This book is dedicated to single mothers.

Made in the USA
Columbia, SC
24 March 2018